Calendar Crafts
Things to Make and Do for Each Month

Written by Carolyn Argyle

Illustrated by Becky J. Radtke

Teaching & Learning Company

1204 Buchanan St., P.O. Box 10
Carthage, IL 62321-0010

This book belongs to

_____

Several of the activities in this book involve preparing, tasting and sharing food items. We urge you to be aware of any food allergies or restrictions your students may have and to supervise these activities diligently. All food-related suggestions are identified with this allergy-alert symbol: ⚠

Please note: small food items (candies, raisins, cereal, etc.) can also pose a choking hazard.

Table of Contents

Dear Teacher or Parent,

This book is filled with more than 100 ideas for inexpensive crafts and recipes to make with children ages 3-8. I have personally tested each and every one of these craft projects. I am the mother of five children, have a degree in Elementary Education and have run a successful home preschool program since 1991. I have used these crafts as a preschool teacher, mother, elementary school volunteer, church worker and den leader.

These activities help teach children many skills including: drawing, cutting, gluing, coloring, folding, cooking, painting, tying and stapling. Other benefits include learning how to follow directions, how to work hard and persevere, how to rise to a challenge and how to expand creativity and thinking skills. Children will also gain increased self-esteem as they take pride in what they can accomplish. Crafts are fun and a great way to bond with your child.

I hope you will find the ideas in this book useful as you work with children. Whether you are an elementary school teacher, preschool teacher, daycare provider, church worker, community worker, home-school teacher or just some-one who wants to share activities at home with your own children, this book is right for you. The wonderful thing about these projects is that, in addition to all the children learn, they end up with something to be proud of, something to bring home and something to keep. Working together is a great way to spend time with children—they learn new things, you learn more about them and everyone has a good time!

Sincerely,

Carolyn

Carolyn Argyle

January

New Year's Confetti

Children learn to use a hole punch in this fun activity.

Give each child a sheet of colored cardstock or construction paper. Have children punch out small pieces of confetti using their hole punches. Trim the edges of the paper occasionally so children can continue punching the middle of the sheet of paper. Put the colored confetti circles in a container to be used for throwing later.

Materials needed for each child:

- colored cardstock or construction paper
- hole punch (regular or designer—e.g. star, heart shapes)

Comb Kazoos

Children learn to make and play a simple musical instrument.

Give each child a 9" x 11" piece of wax paper. Place a comb in the center of the wax paper and fold the wax paper over the teeth of the comb. To play, a child gently places his or her lips over the folded edge of the wax paper and hums. Have children experiment with the kazoos to create the best sound.

Materials needed for each child:

• wax paper
• new, small plastic comb

New Year's Party Hats

Materials needed for each child:

- 1 large sheet colored construction paper (12" x 18")
- crayons
- stapler
- tape
- 1 small sheet construction paper of a different color
- pencil
- ruler
- scissors
- glue
- two 15" lengths of ribbon

This activity will teach children to color, cut, staple and follow directions.

Have each child color designs on the large sheet of construction paper. Tell children to hold the large sheet of construction paper horizontally by its top two corners, then overlap the bottom two corners of the paper to form a cone. Staple the cone to hold its shape. Apply some tape if needed.

Have children cut off the uneven points on the wide end of the cone so the hat will stand up. Use the pencil and ruler to draw a 5" x 6" rectangle on the small sheet of construction paper. Cut out the rectangle. Have children fringe the rectangle on the 6" side. Apply a thick line of glue to the edge of the rectangle opposite the fringe and wrap the glued side around the pointed top of the hat. Bend the fringes outward a little to make a tassel on the hat. Secure it with a staple.

Punch a hole in each side of the hat near the bottom. Insert a 15" ribbon in each hole. Tie knots inside the hat so the ribbon will not pull through the holes. Have children put the hats on and tie them under their chins.

8

New Year's Paper Bag Piñata

Children will learn to cut, hole punch, glue, tie and follow directions. Children will have a blast hitting this piñata and discovering the treats inside.

Have children open the grocery bag and fold the top down toward the inside, about three inches. Make four holes with the hole punch in the top of the bag, one hole on each side. Tie a 24" ribbon or piece of yarn through each hole. Tie the four ribbons together above the bag to make a wide handle.

Cut the crepe paper into strips that fit around the bag. Starting at the bottom of the bag, apply a thin line of glue completely around the bag. Glue a crepe paper strip all the way around the bag. Continue to apply the crepe paper strips, one at a time, until the bag is covered, alternating colors.

Turn the bag upside down. Spread a layer of glue on the bottom. Glue streamers on the bottom so they hang down. Cover the bottom of the piñata with long hanging streamers.

Turn the piñata right side up. Decorate it like a face with eyes, nose and mouth. Hang the piñata up overnight to dry. Then fill it with wrapped candy and small toys.

Hang the piñata up high. Have blindfolded children take turns hitting the piñata with a plastic bat or small broom. When someone finally succeeds in breaking the piñata, let all the children share the treats that come spilling out.

Materials needed:

- paper grocery bag
- hole punch
- ribbon or yarn
- 2 rolls of crepe paper streamers in two different colors
- scissors
- glue
- 2 eyes made from construction paper
- mouth and nose cut from construction paper
- candy and small toys
- blindfold
- plastic baseball bat or small broom

Sock Snowmen

Children from all climates can have fun building a snowman!

Have each child fill a sock with cotton balls or beans up to the cuff. Wrap a rubber band many times around the top of the sock, where the cuff begins. Fold the cuff down to make the snowman's hat. Cut a strip of fabric for a scarf and tie it underneath the heel of the sock to make a head. Glue on the eyes. Cut the nose and mouth from black felt and glue them on. Add buttons.

Materials needed for each child:

- 1 clean white tube sock
- cotton balls or beans
- rubber band
- fabric scrap
- scissors
- googly craft eyes
- black felt (for nose and mouth)
- buttons
- glue

Snowman Sandwiches

Children learn to create a fun and healthy snowman-shaped snack.

Have children cut large circles out of each slice of bread, using the large glass or the crust remover. Spread peanut butter on two slices of bread and jelly or jam on the other two slices. Put the slices together to form two peanut butter-and-jelly sandwiches. Place the two circular sandwiches on a plate, one on top of the other. Use the wheat crackers to make a hat; the baby carrot stick for a nose; and the raisins for eyes, mouth and buttons. Use the medium carrot sticks for arms.

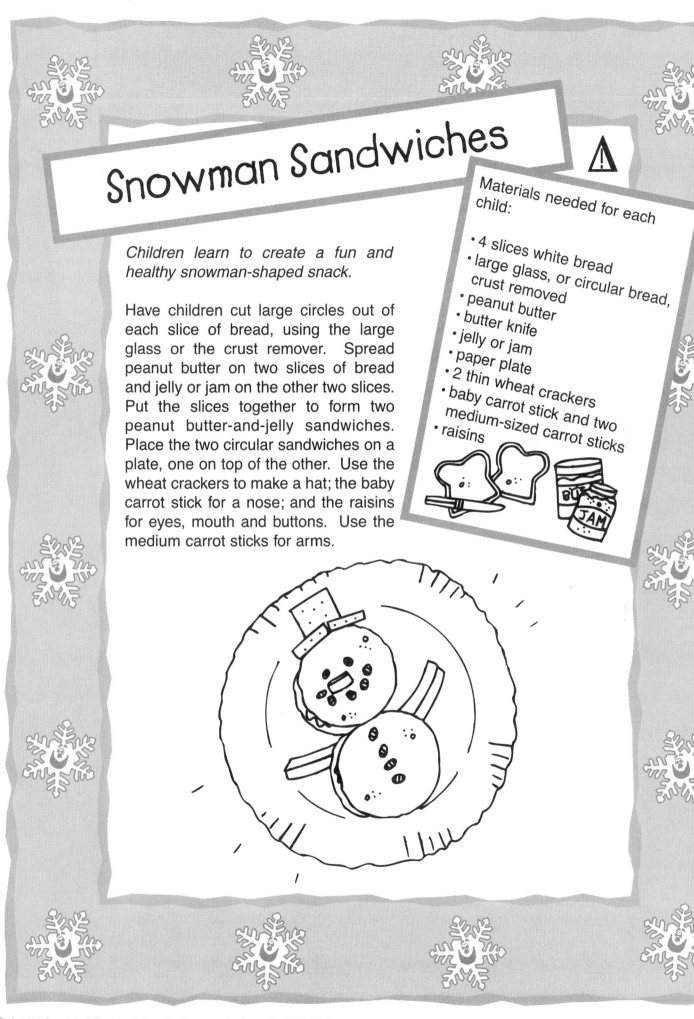

Materials needed for each child:

- 4 slices white bread
- large glass, or circular bread, crust removed
- peanut butter
- butter knife
- jelly or jam
- paper plate
- 2 thin wheat crackers
- baby carrot stick and two medium-sized carrot sticks
- raisins

Puffy Penguins

Children will learn to follow directions by stuffing, taping and gluing together a standing penguin.

For younger children, have the penguin head and body pattern, eyes, bow tie, feet and beak already cut out. Older children may use the patterns to cut out their own pieces. Cut one penguin head and body pattern from black construction paper. Cut two large white eyes and two small black eyes from construction paper. Cut out an orange beak and two orange feet. Cut out a red bow tie.

Fill a lunch sack three-fourths full with old newspapers. Fold down the top and securely tape or staple it closed. Glue the body to the front of the bag. Glue the bow tie to the neck. Glue on the white eyes and the small black eyes inside them. Fold the beak in half, and glue only one side of it to the bag so it opens three-dimensionally. Glue the feet to the bottom of the bag so they stick out just a bit.

Materials needed for each child:

- patterns, page 13
- construction paper (black, white, orange and red)
- scissors
- 1 white lunch sack
- old newspaper
- clear mailing tape or stapler
- glue

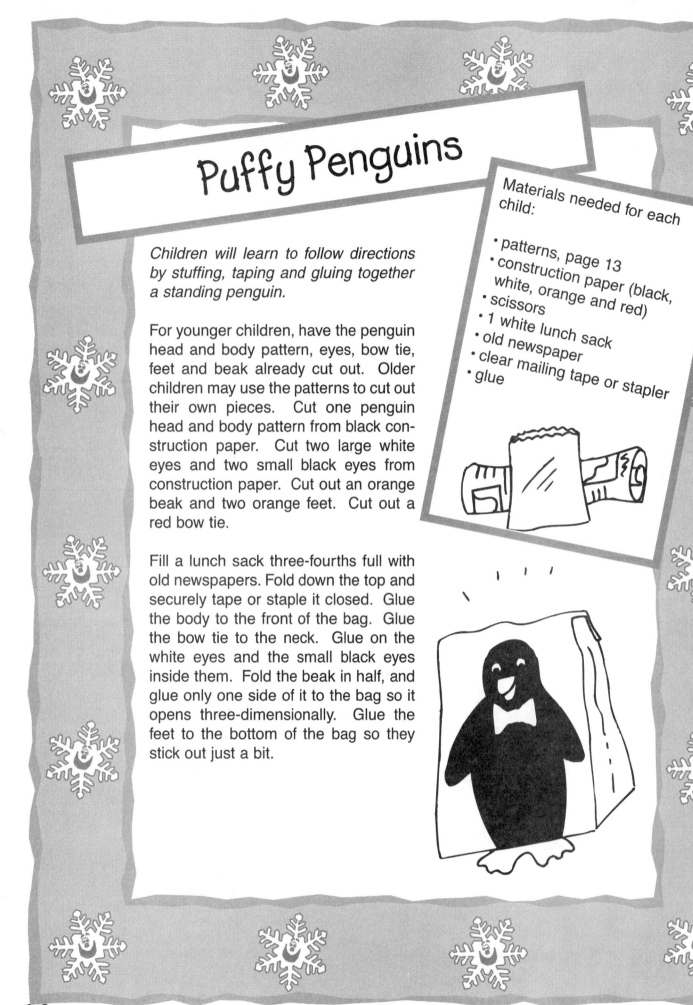

Puffy Penguin Patterns

eye

beak

feet

body

bow tie

Yummy Snowmen

Children will love this delicious upside-down treat!

Place three scoops of vanilla ice cream, one on top of another, on a plate. On the top scoop, make eyes and a mouth with chocolate chips. Make a nose with candy corn. On the middle scoop, make buttons with m & m's™. Put a sugar cone on the snowman's head for a hat. Then turn the snowman upside down and eat him like an ice cream cone.

Materials needed for each child:

- vanilla ice cream
- paper plate
- chocolate chips
- candy corn
- m & m's™
- sugar cone

14

Sugar Cube Igloos

Children will learn patience and perseverance as they build their own sugar cube igloos.

Give each child a paper bowl. Have them turn their bowls upside down on sheets of wax paper. Place a row of sugar cubes along the bottom edge of the bowl, attaching them to the bowl with frosting. Have the children spread white frosting on two sides of each sugar cube and "glue" it on top of the bottom row, forming a second row of sugar cube bricks. Continue until the entire bowl is covered with sugar cube bricks to make an igloo.

Glue cotton balls on the sheet of cardboard to look like snow. Place the igloo, when dry, on the sheet of cardboard. To make the igloo entrance, fold the thin sheet of cardboard over to form a long, narrow, cave-like entrance. Cover it with sugar cubes, attaching them with frosting. Let it dry.

Materials needed for each child (or for the group):

- paper bowl
- wax paper
- sugar cubes
- white frosting
- butter knife
- rectangular sheet of flat cardboard
- cotton balls
- glue
- thin sheet cardboard

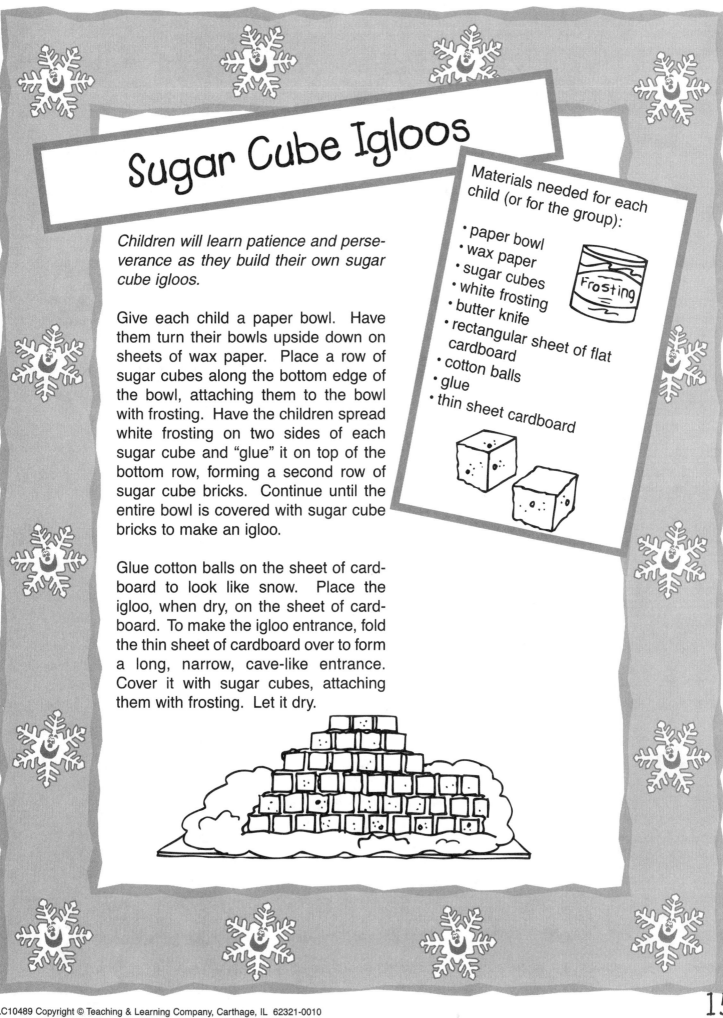

Snow Candy

This is a fun outdoor activity when it snows!

Pour the syrup into the saucepan. Warm the syrup on the stove. (Do not boil.) Take the warm syrup outside to a patch of fresh, clean snow. Pat the snow down a little bit to create a nice, flat surface.

With the wooden spoon, drizzle the warm syrup onto the snow. Watch the syrup harden into homemade candy! Eat the sweet treat.

Materials needed:

- strawberry or blueberry syrup
- saucepan
- wooden spoon

Caution! Supervision required. Be extremely careful when using heat source.

16

Pinecone Bird Feeders

Children will learn to follow directions to create a pinecone bird feeder they can hang outdoors in a tree. Watch the birds enjoy it!

Materials needed for each child:

- pinecone
- yarn
- birdseed
- peanut butter

Have children tie a length of yarn to the top of their pinecones. (Do this for younger children.) Place some peanut butter on a plate, and have children roll their pinecones in it, covering the pinecones. Sprinkle birdseed all over the pinecone. Hang it outdoors and watch the birds enjoy it!

18

Chocolate Necklaces

⚠️

Materials needed for each child:

- 2' sheet plastic wrap
- 8 individually wrapped chocolate candies
- ribbon

Children will learn to follow directions and tie simple knots to create this pretty and delicious necklace.

Tear off a two-foot sheet of plastic wrap. Spread it out on the table. Evenly space chocolate candies down the center with one about every three inches. Fold the plastic wrap in from both sides, covering the candy. Have children tie a piece of ribbon between each piece of candy using a double knot. Tie ribbon on the ends. Tie the ends together forming a necklace for the child to wear—and later eat!

Pop-Out Valentine Cards

Children will use their creativity to decorate this card, cutting, taping, drawing and writing. This will be a fun card to give away on Valentine's Day.

Have children fold a sheet of construction paper, colored paper or cardstock in half twice (or once for a larger card). Let them decorate the front of the card with crayons or markers and whatever words they want to say. (You may need to write the words for younger children.) For a pop-out feature inside, have children cut a 1" x 6" piece of paper and accordion fold it. Tape one end of the folded strip to the right side of the inside of the card. Tape the other end to a small picture (heart, teddy bear, balloon, frog, etc.) the child has drawn, colored and cut out so it "jumps" out of the card. Have children write a message inside the card. Then close the card, being sure to push the pop-out flat inside the card.

Materials needed for each child:

- construction paper, colored paper or cardstock
- scissors
- tape
- markers or crayons

Valentine Rabbits

Children will enjoy assembling this Valentine rabbit.

Cut a large heart from red construction paper for the body. Cut a medium-sized red heart for the head. Cut two small pink hearts for the feet. Cut one very small pink heart for the nose. Cut two pink ears. Have children glue the pieces to a sheet of white construction paper to form a rabbit. They can draw eyes and glue a cotton ball on for the tail. Use white curling ribbon for the whiskers.

Valentine Rabbit Patterns

ears

head

body

nose

feet

22

Paper Plate Valentine Pockets

Children will learn to make a Valentine pocket to hang on the wall, a desk or a bedroom doorknob.

Have children cut one paper plate in half. Place the half plate upside down on top of the whole plate, with the rims lining up at the bottom. Hold them in place and staple them together along the rim. Then punch holes around the top half of the whole plate, about 1" apart. Starting near the top and leaving a 14" tail, lace yarn through the holes of the paper plate. Go across the back to the other side of the plate behind the pocket and continue lacing until meeting the other lace at the top. With the tail, tie a bow at the top for a hanger. Let children decorate the plates and add their names.

Optional: Have children lace the yarn around the entire pocket. This is a little more difficult, since holes are harder to punch through the thickness of two plates.

Materials needed for each child:

- 2 large paper plates
- scissors
- stapler
- hole punch
- red yarn (or other color)
- decorations of your choice (construction paper, stickers, paint, markers, glitter pens, etc.)

Funny Face Valentine Necklaces

Children love wearing jewelry they've made themselves. This was a hit at our second-grade class Valentine's Day party.

Cut the pipe cleaners in half. Have the children make a chain by forming circles from the pipe cleaner stems, twisting the ends together and connecting the links to one another. Alternate red and white rings. Leave the pipe cleaner stems unconnected at either end of the chain.

Cut a two-inch heart shape from a sheet of red foam. Use the hole punch to make a hole on each side of the heart at the top. Insert the unconnected pipe cleaner stems into the heart and twist them closed to complete the necklace. Use glue to create a lovable face complete with googly eyes and pom-pom nose on the heart. To form a smiling mouth, cut a 1¹/₂" long piece from a leftover white pipe cleaner stem and curve it slightly. Let the face dry for 15 minutes, and the necklace is ready to wear.

Materials needed for each child:

- 5 red pipe cleaners
- 6 white pipe cleaners
- scissors
- 1 sheet red foam board
- hole punch
- glue
- 2 googly craft eyes
- 1 small pink pom-pom

Flowerpot Valentines

Each child will love to make this special valentine for a special person.

Have children put a small amount of playdough in the bottom of a miniature flowerpot. Cut small hearts from red construction paper. Write notes on them (I love you, You are nice, etc.). Tape the hearts to the craft sticks. Stick the craft sticks into the playdough inside the flowerpot.

Materials needed for each child:

- miniature flowerpot (found in craft stores)
- playdough
- red construction paper
- scissors
- markers
- wooden craft sticks
- tape

Plaster Heart Refrigerator Magnets

Children will love to paint these heart magnets to give to special people on Valentine's Day.

Mix the plaster with water (twice as much plaster as water) in a small bowl. Pour it into a heart mold. Let it dry for 30 minutes to one hour. Take it out of the mold. Paint the entire heart with red or pink paint. When it's dry, spray it with clear gloss finish. When that's dry, glue a magnet to the back of the heart.

Materials needed for each child:

- plaster of paris
- water
- small dish or bowl
- small heart mold (found in craft stores)
- pink or red acrylic paint
- paintbrush
- high-gloss protective finish (clear glaze spray found at craft stores)
- magnet (found at craft stores)
- glue

Valentine Pizzas

Materials needed:

- large cookie sheets
- cooking spray
- frozen bread dough, thawed
- rolling pin
- tomato sauce, spaghetti sauce or pizza sauce
- spoon
- browned ground beef or pepperoni
- oregano or garlic salt (your preference)
- shredded mozzarella cheese

Children will enjoy creating their own heart pizzas or making these for someone they love. Children will learn to grease a pan, spread and roll dough and top their pizzas.

Grease the pans with the cooking spray. Have children roll the dough out with rolling pins. Using their hands, they can shape the dough into heart shapes on cookie sheets. Pinch up the edges to hold the pizza filling.

Pour the tomato sauce on the dough. Spread it to the edges with a spoon. Spoon ground beef or place pepperoni on the tomato sauce. Sprinkle oregano or garlic salt over it.

Bake in a preheated oven at 425°F for 20 minutes, or until the crust is brown and the pizza is bubbly. (Individual smaller pizzas will take less time.) After the pizzas are browned, remove them from the oven and sprinkle them evenly with cheese. Return them to the oven until the cheese melts.

Valentine Bags

These bags are great for a Valentine's Day party.

Have children decorate the sacks with markers, crayons and/or stickers. Write each child's name on his or her sack. Use the bags for holding party favors or Valentine candy.

Materials needed for each child:

- 1 white or red paper sack (found at craft stores)
- markers or crayons
- Valentine stickers

Valentine's Day Punch

Children will learn how to create a delicious punch for Valentine's Day.

Have children help you make red punch. First fill the pitcher three-fourths full with water. Add one cup of sugar and the flavored drink mix powder. Stir it well. Pour the punch into ice cube trays and freeze. Pour lemon-lime soda pop into glasses and add a few flavored ice cubes. The drinks will turn red. Enjoy!

Materials needed:

- pitcher
- water
- 1 envelope red, flavored drink mix powder
- measuring cup
- sugar
- empty ice cube trays
- drinking glasses
- lemon-lime soda pop

Butterfly Valentines

Materials needed for each child:

- red construction paper
- scissors
- glue
- wooden craft stick
- marker
- pipe cleaner
- tape

Children will enjoy making these valentines. Use string to hang them or glue a magnet to the back of each and put it on the refrigerator.

Cut two hearts out of red paper, about as tall and wide as the craft stick is long. Trim off the pointed end of each heart. Lay the two hearts down so the bottom edges are slightly overlapping each other. Glue them together on the bottom edges. Glue the craft stick onto the hearts, over the glued seam.

Use the marker to draw eyes and a mouth on the craft stick. Write a Valentine's Day message on the wings of the butterfly. Cut two 2" pieces from a pipe cleaner. Tape them on the back of the craft stick to be the butterfly's antenna.

Valentine Pom-Pom Magnets

These are great fun to make and use and easy!

Cut a heart shape from red construction paper (about 2" across). Write a message near the top (I love you, be my valentine, etc.). Glue the pom-pom in the middle of the heart. Glue the eyes on the heart. Stick the magnet strip on the back. Use the heart as a refrigerator magnet.

Materials needed for each child:

- red construction paper
- scissors
- thin black marker
- 1 5" pom-pom (any color)
- glue
- 2 googly craft eyes
- ½" wide flexible strip magnet, cut into 1" piece

Valentine Mouse

This cute little mouse carries a message on its tail.

Cut a heart about 7" tall from white construction paper. Fold the heart lengthwise down the middle. Open it and put tissue paper inside, to stuff it. Cut a 12" length of yarn. Put the end of the yarn about an inch inside the top of the heart. Glue around all edges of the heart and fold it in half, with the yarn tail sticking out. Cut a small heart of red felt. Glue it on the heart mouse near the point, with the point of the red felt facing the point of the large heart and half of the red felt heart on each side of the large heart for ears. Draw a nose, whiskers and an eye on each side of the mouse. Cut a small heart from white or red construction paper. Write a message on it and glue it to the tip of the mouse's tail.

Materials needed for each child:

- construction paper (white and red)
- scissors
- tissue paper
- red yarn
- glue
- red felt
- black marker

Happy Valentine's Day!

Wind Socks

Children will enjoy the March winds as they fly their own wind socks. Children will learn to follow directions, glue, staple, punch holes, tape and decorate.

Have children color a bright design on one side of the white paper. Hold the paper so the long sides are at the top and bottom, and fold the top down one inch. Roll the paper into a cylinder nine inches long with the folded edge on the inside and the colored design on the outside. Glue the ends together.

Cut a 12" crepe paper streamer. Staple it around the bottom edge of the cylinder. Cut four crepe paper streamers, each 24" long. Staple one end of each streamer inside the bottom edge of the cylinder so the streamers hang down.

Use the hole punch to make three holes an equal distance apart around the top edge of the cylinder. Tie one end of a ribbon in each hole. Tie the other end of the three ribbons together to make a single knot. Tie the 24" ribbon to this knot. Hang the wind sock outside to catch the breeze!

Materials needed for each child:

- 9" x 12" white construction paper
- markers or crayons
- glue
- crepe paper streamers
- scissors
- stapler
- hole punch
- narrow crimped paper ribbon, cut into three 10" pieces and one 24" piece

Clothespin Lambs

Children will learn to cut out a shape from a pattern, glue and create a lamb that stands up.

Cut a pattern for a lamb from heavy cardboard. Have children use a pencil to trace around the pattern onto the white cardstock. Cut out the sheep. With the marker, draw an eye, nose and mouth on the sheep (looking at it from a side view). Glue cotton balls to cover the sheep's body. Clip the two clothespins to the legs of the lamb to make it stand up.

Materials needed for each child:

- 1 lamb pattern (from a coloring book or this page, below)
- 1 sheet white cardstock
- pencil
- scissors
- marker
- cotton balls
- glue
- 2 spring-type clothespins

Shamrock Pins

Children will love making this pin and wearing it on St. Patrick's Day. Children will learn to cut from a pattern, sew on a button and glue.

Make a shamrock pattern by drawing three hearts together, then adding a stem. Have each child use a pen or pencil to trace the shamrock on the green felt square. Cut out the shamrock. (You'll need to do this for younger children.) Help children thread the needle and sew a gold button in the middle of the shamrock. (Do this for younger children.) It should only take a few stitches. Use glue to attach the pin backing to the back of the shamrock. Let it dry and the pin is done!

Materials needed for each child:

- green felt, cut into a 2" square
- scissors
- needle
- thread
- 1 gold button
- 1 pin back (sold in craft stores)
- craft glue
- pen or pencil

36

March Lions

Materials needed for each child:

- 8 strips (9" x 1") yellow construction paper
- 8 strips (9" x 1") orange construction paper
- black marker
- 1 large paper plate
- glue

Children will learn to work with patience and perseverance as they curl and glue the mane on this cute lion face. These make nice decorations for the walls or a bulletin board for the month of March.

Show children how to curl the strips of paper by wrapping one around a pencil or marker, then pulling the pencil or marker out. Have children curl all their paper strips. Glue the strips around the rim of the paper plate, with the curls facing in. Have each child draw a face on the lion: eyes, a triangular nose with a line drawn to the mouth, freckles and whiskers.

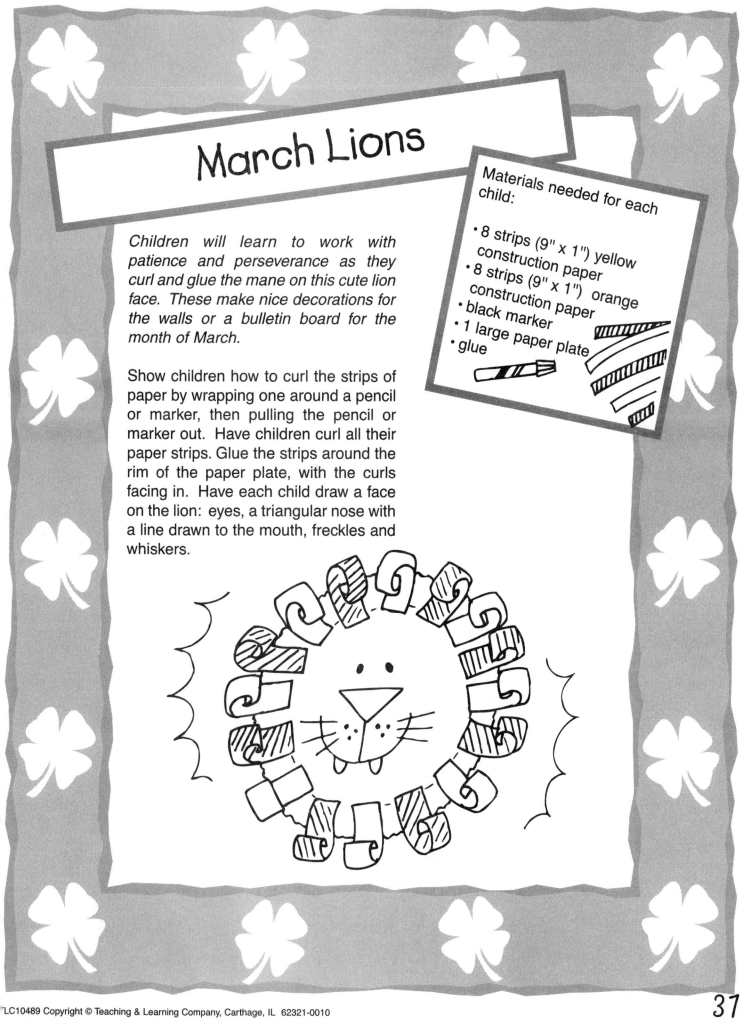

Shamrock Prints

Children will enjoy making shamrock prints. Use them to decorate cards, wrapping paper or bulletin boards.

Cut bell peppers in half and clean out the seeds. Children can dip the cross-sections of the peppers into green paint and press the shamrock prints onto paper.

Materials needed for each child:

• half a bell pepper
• green washable tempera paint
• paper

Shamrock Leprechauns

Materials needed for each child:

- large shamrock cut from green construction paper
- markers or crayons
- 2 strips (6" x 1") green construction paper
- 2 strips (9" x 1") green construction paper
- glue

Children will learn to follow directions, folding paper and drawing a face for this fun little man.

Have each child draw a face on the shamrock. Then have children accordion fold the long and short strips of paper. Glue the short pieces on the shamrock for arms and the longer pieces for legs.

Filter Paper Shamrocks

Children will learn about colors as they create these beautiful shamrocks.

Cut a shamrock shape out of a coffee filter for each child. Mix water and yellow food coloring in a baby food jar or similar container. Do the same with blue food coloring. Let children use eyedroppers or straws to drip colors on the filter shape. The colors will run together and make beautiful shamrocks.

Materials needed for each child:

- 1 coffee filter
- water
- yellow and blue food coloring
- eyedroppers or straws

40

Pot-O-Gold

Children will color and paint this rainbow and pot of gold.

Have children paint their paper tube lengths black. Cut the center from each paper plate half. Have children color the arc like a rainbow. Then slide one end of the "rainbow" into the black paper tube. Glue it in place. The black tube represents a pot of gold at the end of a rainbow! For an added touch, let each child put a line of glue around the top edge of the paper tube and sprinkle on gold glitter or sequins.

Materials needed for each child:

• toilet tissue tube or paper towel tube cut to 2" length
• black washable tempera paint
• 1 paper plate, cut in half
• crayons
• glue

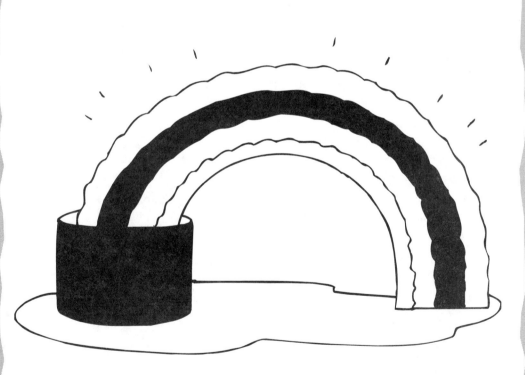

Teddy Bear Cake

Children will love to help you make this delicious and adorable cake!

Mix the cake mix according to the package directions. Spray the two round pans and custard bowl with cooking spray. Pour the cake mix into the pans and bowl. Bake them as directed. Let them cool, and then remove the cakes from the pans. Place one round cake on the sheet pan, and cover it with chocolate frosting for the head. Cut two ear shapes from the other cake. Frost the ears with chocolate frosting and attach them to the head. Place the small cake made in the custard bowl on the center of the face. Cover it with white frosting for the nose. Add a gumdrop for the tip of the nose and licorice for a line leading down to a licorice mouth. Put some white frosting in the middle of each ear. Cut the large marshmallow in half and use them for eyes. Make a pupil in the eyes with chocolate frosting. Cover the whole cake with colored coconut "fur," if desired.

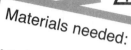

Materials needed:

- cake mix (any flavor)
- 2 round cake pans
- 1 small custard bowl
- cooking spray
- 1 large sheet pan
- 1 can chocolate frosting
- 1 can white frosting
- large gumdrop for nose
- red string licorice
- 1 large marshmallow
- coconut, colored brown with food coloring (optional)

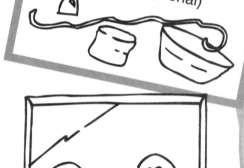

Yum!

42

Shamrock Necklaces

Children will love wearing this necklace they've made themselves and it will protect them from being pinched for not wearing green on St. Patrick's Day!

Have each child make a chain by forming circles from the pipe cleaners, twisting the ends together, and connecting the links to one another. Leave the pipe cleaners at either end of the chain unconnected.

Use the hole punch to make a hole on either side of the shamrock at the top. Insert the unconnected pipe cleaner stems into the shamrock and twist them closed to complete the necklace. Use glue to add googly eyes and pom-pom nose for a lovable face on the shamrock. To form a smiling mouth, cut a short piece from leftover pipe cleaner and curve it slightly. Glue it to the shamrock. Let the shamrock dry for 15 minutes, and the necklace is ready to wear.

Materials needed for each child:

- 9 green pipe cleaners, cut in half
- scissors
- 2" shamrock shape cut from green foam
- hole punch
- glue
- 2 googly craft eyes
- 1 small white pom-pom

44

Milk Jug Easter Baskets

Children will enjoy making these darling Easter baskets.

Cut a large circle in the side of the milk jug without the handle (near the bottom) for the mouth. Have children glue cotton balls to cover the milk jug. Cut two ears from white construction paper and two inner ears from pink construction paper. Glue the pink inner ears on top of the white ears, then glue the ears to the top of the milk carton. Cut circles from blue construction paper for eyes, smaller black circles for pupils and a pink circle for the nose. Cut six strips of black construction paper for whiskers. Glue them all on the face. Fill the basket with Easter grass and seasonal treats.

Materials needed for each child:

- 1 clean empty gallon milk jug
- cotton balls
- glue
- construction paper (pink, blue, black and white)

Rabbit Sacks

These sacks make great bags for collecting Easter eggs at an Easter egg hunt.

While the lunch sack is still folded up, draw ears at the top of it. Cut around the ears. Cut small ears from pink construction paper and glue them in the center of the ears on the sack. Cut two eyes from white construction paper and two smaller eyes from black construction paper. Glue the black eyes inside the white eyes, then glue them on the bag. Cut a triangle nose from pink construction paper and glue it on the bag. Draw whiskers, a smile and freckles with the marker. Glue the cotton ball on the back of the bag for the tail. Make a handle out of construction paper (double thickness) and staple it on.

Materials needed for each child:

- brown or white lunch sack
- scissors
- construction paper (pink, white and black)
- glue
- marker
- cotton ball

Egg Carton Easter Baskets

Here is another way to carry those precious Easter eggs!

Cut a section of four eggcups together from an egg carton. Poke a pipe cleaner through one side of the egg carton section and twist it to secure it. Do the same to the other three sides with pipe cleaners. Twist the four pipe cleaners together at the top to make a handle. Fill the egg cups with Easter grass and candy.

Materials needed for each child:

- egg carton
- 4 pipe cleaners
- Easter grass
- candy (such as jelly beans)

Living Easter Baskets

Children will enjoy planting grass and watching it grow in this fun basket that can also hold Easter eggs and serve as an Easter decoration.

Decorate the bottom of the half-gallon milk carton with construction paper shapes or Easter stickers. Fill the container with potting soil and sprinkle an ample amount of grass seed on it. (Rye seed grows fastest.) Keep the plants in a well-lit space and water them a little each day. After the grass grows a few inches, put Easter eggs inside the basket.

Materials needed for each child:

- 1 clean cardboard or plastic half-gallon milk carton, cut in half (Discard the top half with the pouring spout.)
- poster board or cardstock
- construction paper or Easter stickers
- glue
- stapler
- potting soil
- grass seed

Spring Treasures Totes

Materials needed for each child:

- 1 paper plate
- crayons or markers
- stapler
- 1 pipe cleaner
- hole punch

Children will enjoy making this simple tote and using it when going on a spring nature walk. Have children fill their totes with special treasures (wild flowers, rocks, leaves, etc.).

Have children decorate the back of the paper plate with crayons or markers. Fold the paper plate in half, then unfold it. (step 1) Fold each side in to meet in the center of the plate. (step 2)

Unfold the plate again. Fold the plate along the center, then fold the ends in. Staple the ends to make the tote. (step 3) Punch two holes at the top. Attach a pipe cleaner for a handle. (step 4)

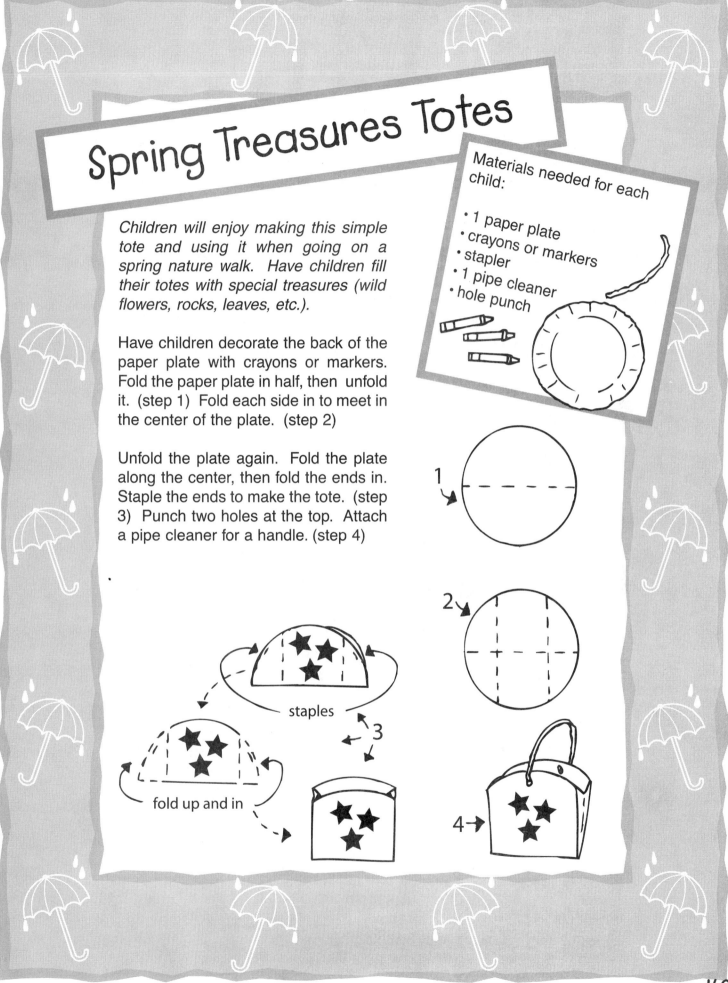

1

2

staples

fold up and in

3

4

Marshmallow Treat Egg Nests

Children will learn to mold their rice crisp treats into nest shapes. They may fill the birds' nests with egg-shaped candy, then eat it up!

Prepare one batch of rice crisp marshmallow treats. Give each child about half a cup of the mixture. Have children shape the treat into nests. They can fill the cooled nests with green coconut (optional) and jelly beans or chocolate eggs.

Materials needed for each child:

- ¹⁄₂ cup rice crisp marshmallow treats mixture (recipe on most boxes of rice crisp cereal)
- small amount of green-tinted coconut (optional: since some young children do not like coconut)
- jelly beans or chocolate eggs

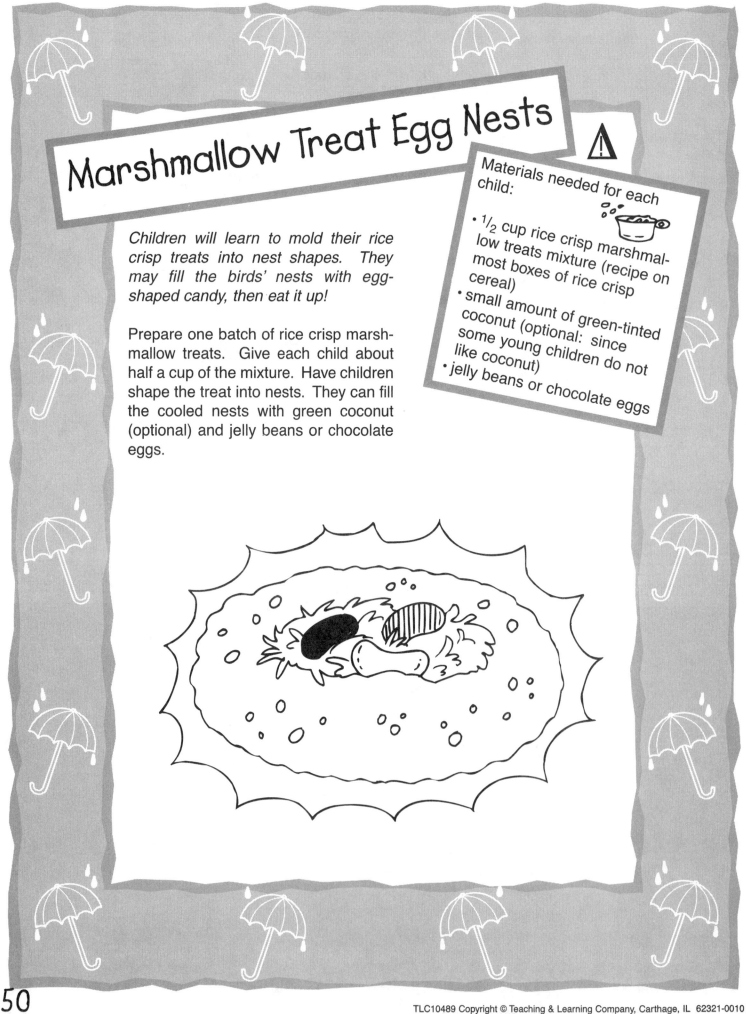

Bird Nests

⚠

Materials needed for each child:

- $\frac{1}{3}$ c butterscotch morsels (milk chocolate, semi-sweet or white chocolate morsels will also work)
- 1 c chow mein noodles
- wax paper
- candy robin's eggs

Children will learn some cooking skills as they make these genuine-looking bird nests. Yummy!

Melt butterscotch morsels in a microwave-safe bowl. Add chow mein noodles and gently mix. Shape the mixture into a circle on wax paper. Use a large spoon to make an indention in the center of the mixture to form a nest. Let the nest harden, then add candy robin's eggs.

Popcorn Easter Eggs

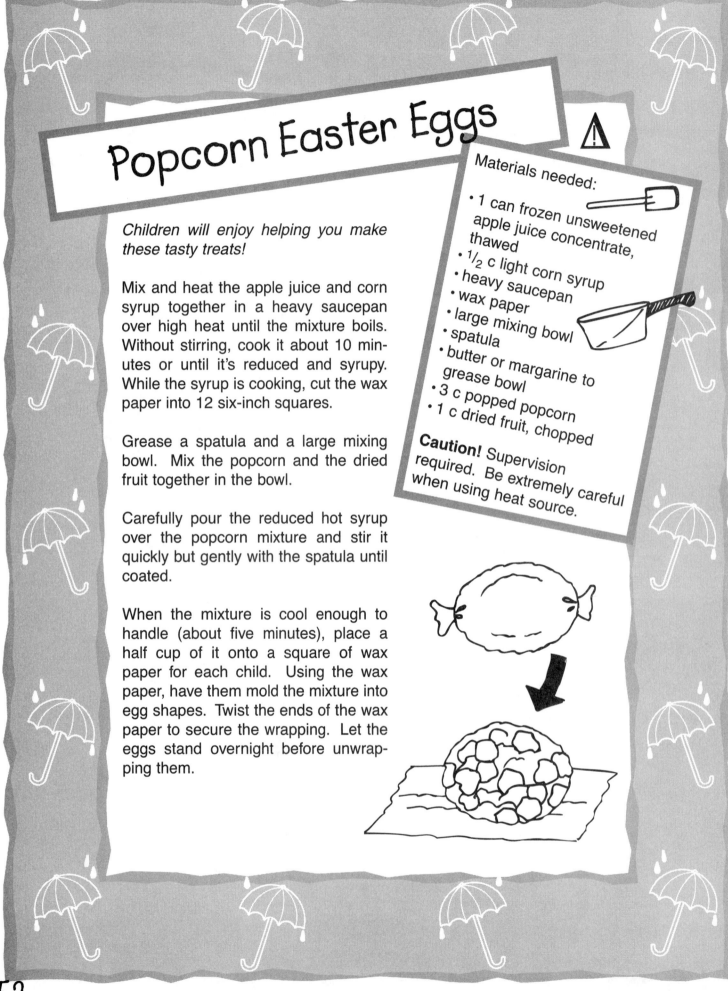

Children will enjoy helping you make these tasty treats!

Mix and heat the apple juice and corn syrup together in a heavy saucepan over high heat until the mixture boils. Without stirring, cook it about 10 minutes or until it's reduced and syrupy. While the syrup is cooking, cut the wax paper into 12 six-inch squares.

Grease a spatula and a large mixing bowl. Mix the popcorn and the dried fruit together in the bowl.

Carefully pour the reduced hot syrup over the popcorn mixture and stir it quickly but gently with the spatula until coated.

When the mixture is cool enough to handle (about five minutes), place a half cup of it onto a square of wax paper for each child. Using the wax paper, have them mold the mixture into egg shapes. Twist the ends of the wax paper to secure the wrapping. Let the eggs stand overnight before unwrapping them.

Materials needed:

- 1 can frozen unsweetened apple juice concentrate, thawed
- $\frac{1}{2}$ c light corn syrup
- heavy saucepan
- wax paper
- large mixing bowl
- spatula
- butter or margarine to grease bowl
- 3 c popped popcorn
- 1 c dried fruit, chopped

Caution! Supervision required. Be extremely careful when using heat source.

Stained Glass Windows

A decorative Easter window!

Cover the work area with newspaper. Peel the paper off the crayons. Using the pencil sharpener, scrape the crayons into thin shavings over a bowl. (Avoid thick shavings.) Mix the colored shavings together.

Cut two pieces of wax paper the same size. Sprinkle the shavings over one piece of wax paper, leaving the edges uncovered.

Place the second piece of wax paper over the first. Have an adult gently slide the warm iron over the wax paper. Stop ironing when the shavings have melted together. Let it cool.

Trim the edges of the wax paper to make a square. Punch a hole near the top of the square. Put a length of ribbon through the hole, and tie the ends together. Hang the stained glass squares in a window.

Materials needed:

- old newspapers
- old crayons
- pencil sharpener
- small bowl
- scissors
- wax paper
- iron, set on low heat
- hole punch
- ribbon

Caution! Supervision required. Be extremely careful when using the iron.

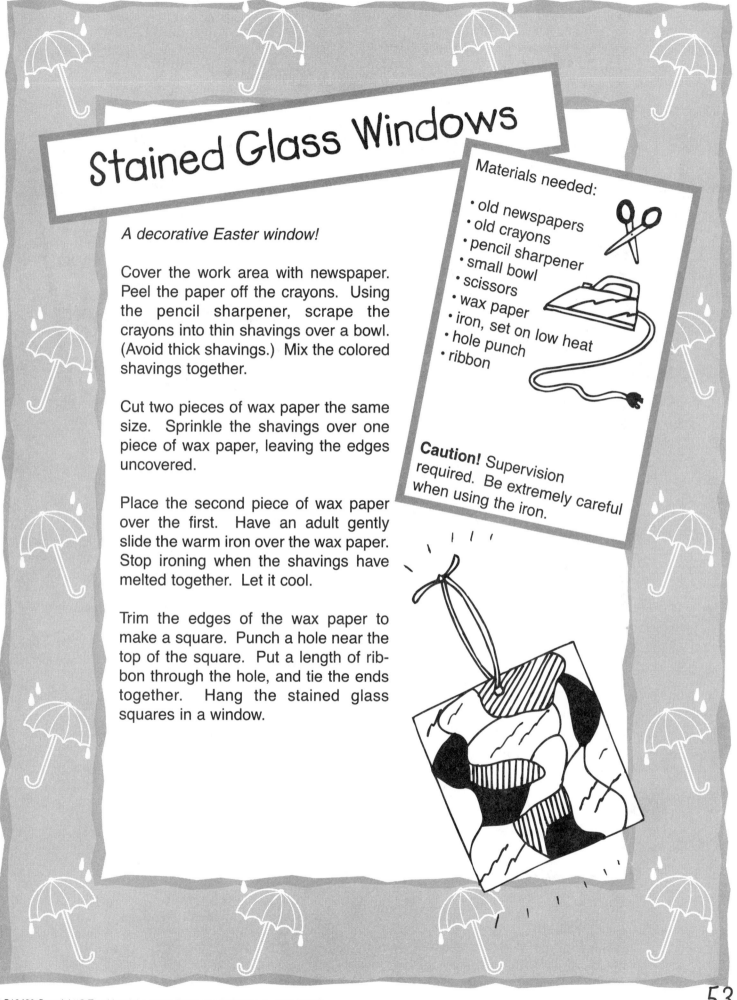

Pasta Egg Nests

Children will learn cooking skills as they help you mix the ingredients and fill the large pasta shells for a delicious and nutritious treat! Serves 12.

Have children help mix the eggs, relish, salt and pepper in a bowl. Fill each nest (shell) with the egg mixture.

⚠

Materials needed:

• 12 jumbo pasta shells, cooked, then rinsed with cold water
• 6 hard-cooked eggs, peeled and chopped
• 1/2 c mayonnaise
• 3 tbsp sweet pickle relish
• 1/4 tsp salt
• 1/8 tsp black pepper

Bunny Cards

Materials needed for each child:

- pattern, page 56
- 1 sheet light blue construction paper
- pencil (for tracing pattern)
- scissors
- black marker or crayons
- white paper
- glue
- pink cotton

Children will love making this card, writing a message inside and giving it to someone special.

Fold the construction paper in half. Trace the rabbit pattern onto the blue paper, keeping the back of the bunny against the fold. Cut it out as shown—leaving it connected at the fold. Have children draw an eye and mouth on the bunny. Cut three strips of white paper for whiskers. Glue the whiskers on the bunny, crossing over each other as shown. Glue the pink cotton ball on the bunny for the tail. Have children write a special Easter message inside.

Happy Easter Grandma! ♡ Min

Bunny Card Pattern

Fold. Do not cut.

Fold. Do not cut.

Happy Handy Ducks

Children will fold, trace, cut and assemble this darling duck.

Using the pattern, cut the duck body from yellow construction paper. Have children trace their hands onto the yellow construction paper and cut them out to use for wings. Using the patterns, cut the bill and two feet from orange construction paper. Cut two white circles for eyes and color black pupils inside. Glue the eyes on the duck. Fold the beak in half and glue it on the duck. Glue on the feet, then attach the hands (wings) with brads to both sides of the duck.

Materials needed for each child:

• patterns, page 58
• construction paper (yellow and orange)
• pencil
• scissors
• white paper
• black crayon
• glue
• 2 brads

Happy Handy Duck Patterns

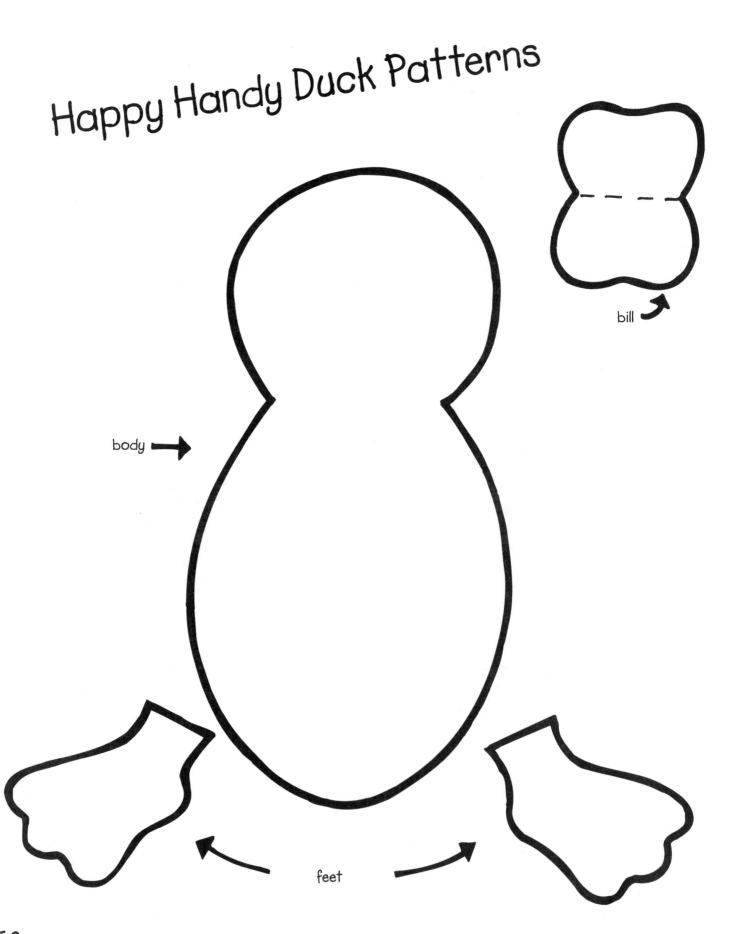

bill

body

feet

May

Mother's Day Drawer Sachets

Children will have fun choosing the fabric, scents and ribbon to make these elegant drawer sachets to give on Mother's Day.

Let each child choose a fabric square. Fill it with two tablespoons of the child's choice of fabric sachet (apples and cinnamon, black cherry, etc.). Bring up the sides of the fabric to the center and tie them with a ribbon to enclose the sachet filling.

Materials needed for each child:

- 1 6" x 6" fabric square
- 2 tbsp fragrant sachet powder (sold in envelopes) or dried lavender
- ribbon

Roll of Sweets for Mom

Children will enjoy making this delicious gift for mother, using their fine motor skills to fill, tie and decorate.

Have children use stickers to decorate three sheets of pink tissue paper. Then they fill the cardboard tube with wrapped candies. They wrap the tube with the decorated tissue paper, twist the ends and tie each end with red rickrack.

Materials needed for each child:

- 3 sheets pink tissue paper
- small heart stickers
- 1 cardboard tube (toilet tissue tube or paper towel tube cut in half)
- wrapped candies
- 2 lengths red rickrack

Hand-Painted Wrapping Paper

Children will enjoy making their own wrapping paper using sponges of various shapes (flowers, stars, teddy bears, bugs, etc.). This makes great paper for wrapping Mom's gift.

Put some paint of each color on a paper plate. Have the child dip a sponge shape into the paint, then press it onto the white newsprint. Have them create designs to cover the wrapping paper.

Materials needed for each child:

- washable tempera paint in various colors
- 1 paper plate
- sponges, cut in small shapes
- 1 large sheet white newsprint

62

Handprint Pop-Up Cards

Children will trace their hands to decorate this special card for Mother.

Have children fold a sheet of construction paper in half twice to create a card. Decorate the front with shapes cut from construction paper, or color it with markers or crayons. Write a message on the inside of the card. Have each child trace a hand on another sheet of colored paper and cut it out. Cut out a long narrow strip of paper and accordion fold it. Tape or glue one end of the strip to the inside (right) of the card and the other end to the back of the hand. Hold the hand down and close the card. The hand will "jump out" when the card is opened.

Materials needed for each child:

• several sheets colored construction paper
• markers or crayons
• scissors
• tape or glue
• stick

Cinnamon French Toast

Mom and Grandma will love this when it's served by your students at a special brunch. Serves four to six.

Beat eggs with water, sugar and cinnamon. Dip bread slices in the egg mixture. Brown both sides of the bread slices in oil on a griddle. You may cut shapes out of the bread (flowers, hearts) using cookie cutters before dipping and browning them.

⚠️

Materials needed for two:

- small shallow bowl
- 2 eggs
- 2 tbsp water
- 1 tsp sugar
- $\frac{1}{4}$ tsp cinnamon
- egg beater
- 4-6 bread slices
- griddle pan or electric skillet
- cooking oil
- spatula

Caution! Supervision required. Be extremely careful when using heat source.

Decorated Clothespin Chip Clips

Children will love making these handy chip clips for gifts for Mother's Day.

If they're using wooden clothespins, have children paint them first. Colored plastic clothespins need no painting. Have each child choose and paint a wooden shape. Let it dry.

Glue the wooden shape on the top of the clothespin (the clip end).

Clip the clothespin to this poem typed on colored cardstock and cut out with decorative scissors:

Materials needed for each child:

- 1 wooden or plastic spring-type clothespin
- acrylic paint
- paintbrush
- small wooden shapes: hearts, butterflies, flowers, frogs, turtles, teddy bears, etc. (available at craft stores)
- copy of poem (below)

Every day, most lovingly,
You open bags to nourish me.
Use this clip for the bags you store:
Chips, pretzels, crackers and more.
Every time I take a bite
I'll know your love is holding me tight!

Chip

Decorated Plastic Bag Dispensers

A fun and useful gift to make for Mom!

Children wrap empty facial tissue boxes with wrapping paper. Cut out the hole to make an opening. Glue rick-rack trim around the hole and along the edges of the box for decoration. Mom can keep her empty plastic grocery bags in this handy container.

Materials needed for each child:

- large empty facial tissue box (rectangular)
- wrapping paper
- scissors
- tape
- braided rickrack trim (optional)
- glue

Flower Pincushions

Kids will love making this handy pin-cushion for Mom.

Have children glue a piece of green felt (which you have cut to fit) around the yogurt container. Cut flower petals from other colors of felt. Have children glue the flower petals around the inside edge of the container, so they are sticking out.

Cover the Styrofoam™ ball with fabric and secure it with a rubber band. Insert the ball into the container until it's stuck. Poke a few pins in the covered ball for starters.

Materials needed for each child:

- 1 clean plastic yogurt container, washed and dried
- felt, green and other spring colors
- glue
- scissors
- Styrofoam™ ball, slightly larger than the opening of the yogurt container
- fabric scraps
- rubber band
- straight pins for sewing

May Day Flower Bouquets

Children will follow directions to make this little flower basket.

Fold the construction paper into a cone shape. Trim the top evenly. Staple the sides of the cone together. Tape along the side to seal the seam. Punch a hole on either side at the top of the cone. Insert one end of the pipe cleaner into the hole and twist it to fasten it. Do the same with the other end of the pipe cleaner to form a handle. Fill the cone with flowers.

Materials needed for each child:

- 1 sheet colored construction paper
- scissors
- stapler
- tape
- hole punch
- pipe cleaner
- flowers (fresh or silk)

Heart Cakes

Here is a special cake to make for Mother's Day.

Make small cakes using a heart-shaped cake pans. Have children cover their cakes with pink frosting. Then they can decorate their cakes any way they wish using sprinkles, candy, coconut, marshmallows and so on.

Materials needed for each child:

- small heart-shaped cake
- pink frosting
- plastic knife
- assorted sprinkles, candies, coconut, marshmallows, etc., for decorating

Summer Door Hangers

Materials needed for each child:

- colored foam door hangers (available at craft stores)
- foam stickers (various shapes and alphabet letters)
- marker

Kids will love to protect their daydreaming dens or decorate their doors with this personalized door hanger. These are also perfect for a summer preschool class reunion.

Have children decorate their door hangers with foam stickers of their choice. They can use foam letters for their initials or use markers to write their names (Crystal's Room) or messages (No girls allowed!).

Bow Tie Dinner Napkins

Materials needed for each child:

• ruler
• construction paper
• scissors
• pen
• 1 cloth napkin
• tape

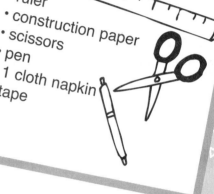

Children can honor Dad, Grandpa or a favorite uncle by setting the dinner table with this decorative napkin.

Cut a 1" x 4" strip of construction paper. Write *Happy Father's Day!* on one side of the paper strip, then set it aside. Fold the napkin in half to form a rectangle (step 1) then in half again to form a square (step 2). Squeeze the napkin in the middle, wrap the paper strip around it with the greeting facing inward and tape the strip in place. Fan the edges of the napkin out to resemble a bow tie (step 3). Place a finished napkin in the center of an empty plate. Tell the guest of honor to remove the paper band from the napkin to read the message before using the napkin.

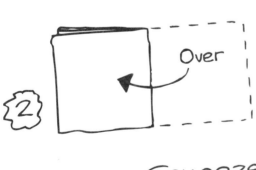

Over ②

Squeeze...
Wrap...
Fan!

Dad's Bookmark

Children will enjoy making this special bookmark for Dad.

Cut the cardboard into a bookmark shape. Have children cut small pictures from magazines of things Dad likes. Glue them on the bookmark. Cover the bookmark with clear, self-adhesive plastic to ensure durability.

Materials needed for each child:

- piece of lightweight card-board
- scissors
- pictures of things Dad likes cut from magazines
- glue
- clear, self-adhesive paper for laminating

For you, Dad!

Mud Pie Brownies

These are fun to make and delicious, too. They're especially appropriate when a summer thunderstorm prohibits outdoor play.

Have children help you make the brownies following instructions on the boxed mix. When cool, spread marshmallow cream on top. Spread chocolate frosting on top of the marshmallow cream. Delicious!

Materials Needed:

- brownie mix (with ingredients listed on box)
- cake pan
- 1 jar marshmallow cream
- 1 container chocolate frosting
- spatula

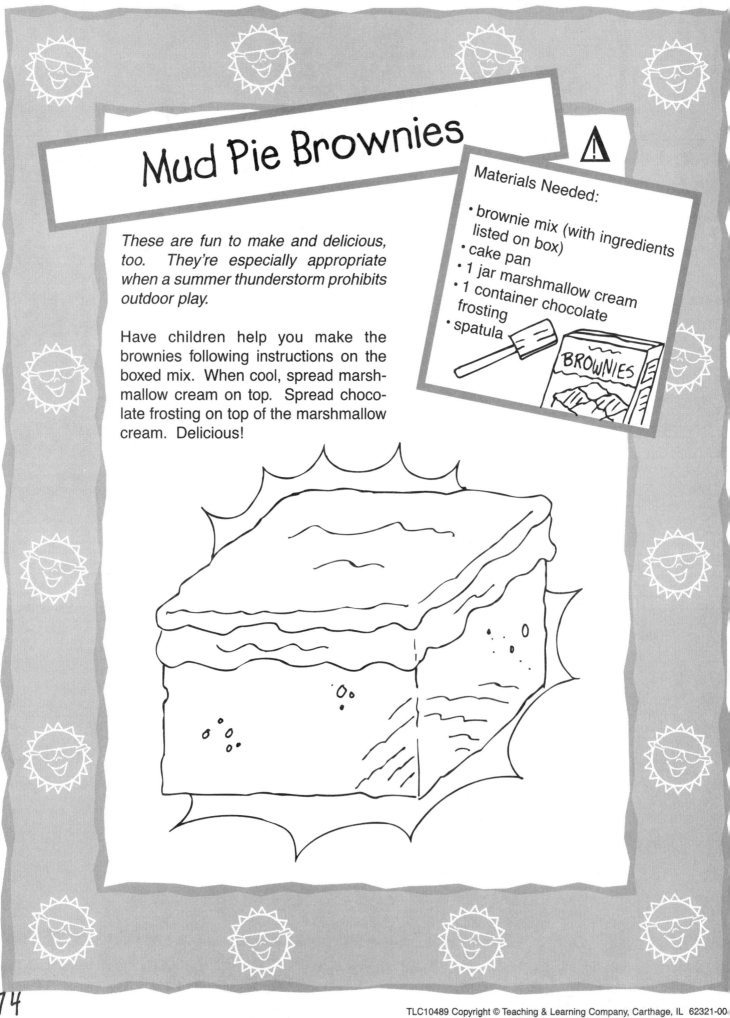

74

Pom-Poms

Materials needed for each child:

- old newspaper
- scissors
- masking tape

Kids love to make these pom-poms, then use them as they pretend to be cheerleaders or shake them as they skip, dance or march to music.

Have children cut the newspaper into several long, thin strips. Gather the strips together and tape them in the center. Fold the strips in half, and bind the folded end with several layers of masking tape.

Collage Pencil Holders for Father's Day

This activity will encourage each child to make a thoughtful gift for a special man on Father's Day.

Have each child look through old magazines to find things that remind him or her of dad or another special man in the family. Have them cut out these pictures and glue them to the juice can, covering it, to make a decorative pencil holder.

Materials needed for each child:

• old magazines
• scissors
• 1 juice can, washed and dried
• glue

Doughnut Sundaes for Father's Day

Children will love to make this deli-cious-looking treat for Father's Day.

Put a doughnut on the center of a small plate. Add a scoop of ice cream in the center of the doughnut. Drizzle a little chocolate syrup on top. Add whipped cream, a cherry and nuts.

Materials needed for each child:

• 1 small paper plate or bowl
• 1 doughnut
• 1 scoop of ice cream
• chocolate syrup
• whipped cream
• cherries
• nuts (optional)

Turtles

Children will enjoy play with these turtles after they have decorated them with personal touches.

Have each child cut out a turtle shape (as shown) from green cardstock. (You may want to provide a simple pattern.) Have the child use crayons or markers to decorate the bottom of a paper bowl like a turtle shell. Glue the bowl upside down onto the body of the turtle. Let it dry. Draw a face on the turtle. Punch a hole at the top of the turtle's head. Thread yarn through the hole and tie it to make a leash. Children can drag their turtles behind them wherever they go!

Materials needed for each child:

- green cardstock
- scissors
- 1 paper bowl
- crayons or markers
- hole punch
- 3' length of yarn, string or ribbon

Kids' Ice Cream

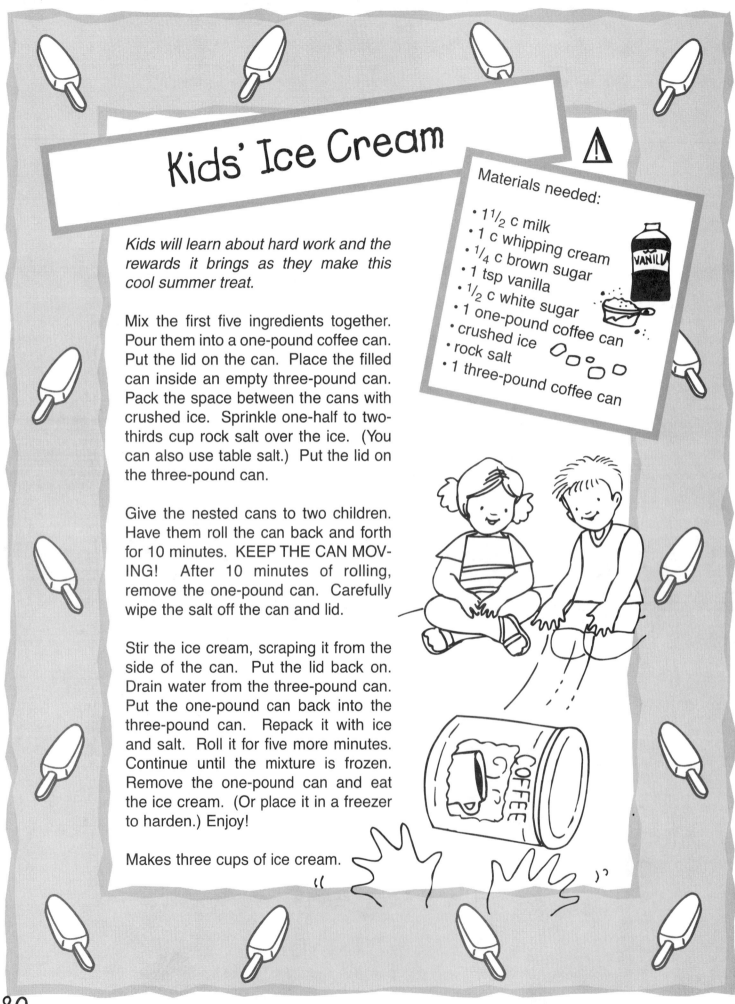

Kids will learn about hard work and the rewards it brings as they make this cool summer treat.

Mix the first five ingredients together. Pour them into a one-pound coffee can. Put the lid on the can. Place the filled can inside an empty three-pound can. Pack the space between the cans with crushed ice. Sprinkle one-half to two-thirds cup rock salt over the ice. (You can also use table salt.) Put the lid on the three-pound can.

Give the nested cans to two children. Have them roll the can back and forth for 10 minutes. KEEP THE CAN MOVING! After 10 minutes of rolling, remove the one-pound can. Carefully wipe the salt off the can and lid.

Stir the ice cream, scraping it from the side of the can. Put the lid back on. Drain water from the three-pound can. Put the one-pound can back into the three-pound can. Repack it with ice and salt. Roll it for five more minutes. Continue until the mixture is frozen. Remove the one-pound can and eat the ice cream. (Or place it in a freezer to harden.) Enjoy!

Makes three cups of ice cream.

Materials needed:

- 1½ c milk
- 1 c whipping cream
- ¼ c brown sugar
- 1 tsp vanilla
- ½ c white sugar
- 1 one-pound coffee can
- crushed ice
- rock salt
- 1 three-pound coffee can

Homemade Butter

⚠

Materials needed for each child:

- ½ pt whipping cream
- yellow food coloring (optional)
- small jar with lid
- ⅛ tsp salt

Delicious when served on saltines for snacktime.

Place the first two ingredients in a jar. Put the lid on the jar and make sure it's secure. Let children take turns shaking the jar until butter forms. Strain the butter and wash it under cold running water. Stir in a small amount of salt.

Scones

Children will enjoy making this easy variation of a traditional quick bread.

Let each child roll a bread dough ball into a pancake shape. Fry it in an electric skillet in hot oil. Turn it over when one side is brown. Children may top their scones with honey or powdered sugar. Delicious!

Materials needed:

• 2" ball frozen bread dough, thawed, for each child
• oil
• electric skillet
• honey or powdered sugar

Caution! Supervision required. Be extremely careful when using heat source.

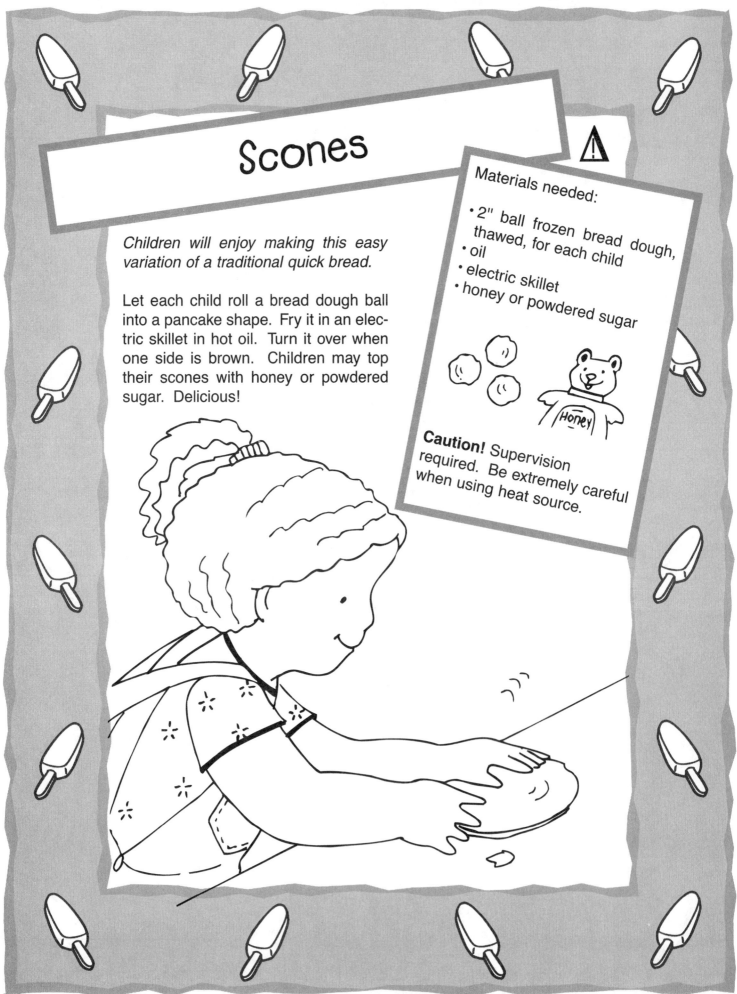

82

Jungle Trail Mix

Children can help mix this healthy treat for a great snack anytime!

Mix all the ingredients in a large bowl. Store it in an airtight container. Makes 11$\frac{1}{2}$ cups.

Materials needed:

- 2 c apple cinnamon toasted oat cereal
- 2 c toasted oat cereal
- 2 c honey nut toasted oat cereal
- 1$\frac{1}{2}$ c animal crackers
- 1$\frac{1}{2}$ c pretzel twists
- 1$\frac{1}{2}$ c cheese-flavored snack crackers
- $\frac{1}{2}$ c assorted fruit snack shapes or gummy candy shapes

Animal Crackers

Gummy Fruit

Hot Air Balloons

Materials needed for each child:

- 1 balloon
- old newspaper
- flour
- water
- acrylic paint
- paintbrush
- string
- empty strawberry basket

Clear blue summer skies invite flights of fancy!

Blow up the balloon. Have each child cover a balloon with newspaper strips dipped into a flour and water paste. Let it dry. Paint the ball shape with acrylic paint to look like a hot air balloon. Let it dry. Poke two holes near the bottom of the balloon on each side (four total). Thread the string through and tie it, leaving a long tail. Tie the four strings to the strawberry basket. Poke two holes near the top of the ball and thread a string through for hanging.

84

Homemade Rubber Stamps

Children love to use rubber stamps, and now they can make their own!

Have children draw stamp designs on paper and cut them out. Place their patterns on the cloth side of foam shoe insoles and trace them. Cut out the shapes.

Brush rubber cement over wood blocks and glue the foam cutouts on them. Press the stamps in the inkpad and stamp away!

Materials needed for each child:

- scrap paper
- fabric foam shoe insoles
- scissors
- rubber cement
- wood blocks
- inkpad

Fabric Crayon Transfers

This is a fun way for children to create their own designs on fabric (jeans, jackets, aprons, T-shirts, place mats, pillowcases, etc.).

Materials needed:

- non-glossy drawing paper
- fabric crayons
- old newspaper
- 1 fabric garment or accessory per child
- iron (hot—no steam)

Caution! Supervision required. Be extremely careful when using the iron.

Have children draw creative designs on non-glossy drawing paper, then color the designs with fabric crayons. (Fabric crayons seem somewhat muted on paper, but transfer brilliantly.)

Prepare an ironing surface by laying clean paper over several layers of newspaper. Set the iron on the cotton setting. A hot, dry (NO STEAM) iron is necessary for an effective transfer.

Place the fabric on the newspaper on the ironing surface. Lay the paper design facedown on the fabric. Place a clean sheet of paper between the iron and the paper design to protect the fabric and to keep the iron from becoming soiled. When transferring a design to clothing, before ironing, insert enough paper between the front and back of the garment to prevent the colors from transferring through to the opposite side of the garment.

Iron with a slow, steady pressure over the entire back of the paper. (Don't hurry or the design will blur.) Check carefully to see that the fabric is not scorching and all the colors have been transferred. Remove the design paper carefully. The paper design can be colored again if another transfer is desired.

Decorated fabrics may be machine-washed, using warm water on the gentle cycle. Do not bleach or dry the fabric in a dryer. The transferred image on the synthetic fabric will remain permanent even after laundering.

Fishbowl Gelatin

This is a delicious, fishy-looking treat!

Make the gelatin according to the package directions. Put it in the refrigerator for 20 minutes. Remove the gelatin from the refrigerator. Gently stir in the candy fish, then spoon the gelatin into small, clear cups. Return it to the refrigerator until it sets; then serve it.

Materials needed:

- 1 package gelatin, any flavor
- 20 candy gummy fish
- 1 small clear plastic cup for each child

Cereal Necklaces

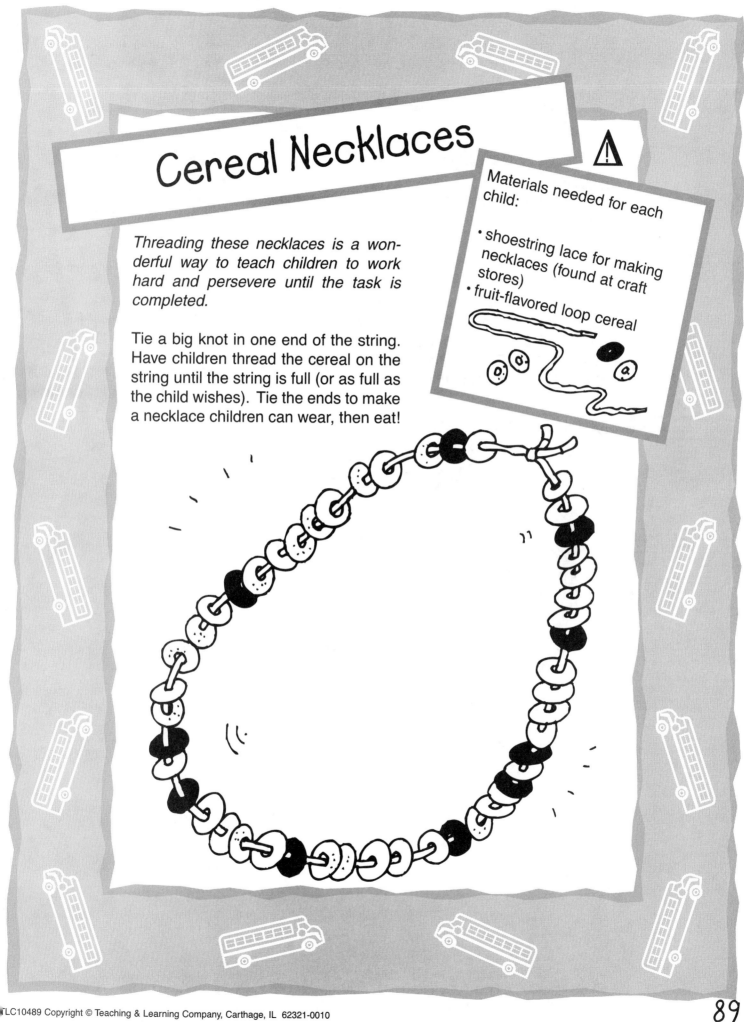

Threading these necklaces is a wonderful way to teach children to work hard and persevere until the task is completed.

Tie a big knot in one end of the string. Have children thread the cereal on the string until the string is full (or as full as the child wishes). Tie the ends to make a necklace children can wear, then eat!

Materials needed for each child:

- shoestring lace for making necklaces (found at craft stores)
- fruit-flavored loop cereal

Summer Scrunchies

These fabric scrunchies make fun gifts for friends or sisters.

Have children select 15 fabric strips of their choice and tie each one to the elastic hair band. A single, tight knot is all that is needed. After all the strips are tied on, the hair ribbon is finished!

Materials needed for each child:

- 1 plain elastic hair band
- 15 strips of fabric (7½" x ¾")

Taffy Pull

Too hot to go outside? Have an indoor party with this sweet treat.

In a heavy saucepan combine honey, sugar and cream. Cook over low heat, stirring until the sugar is dissolved. Continue cooking, stirring as little as possible. When the mixture reaches the hard ball stage (260°F), remove it from the heat and pour it into a shallow, buttered 9" x 13" pan. Turn the edges in with a spatula to prevent the candy from hardening. When it's cool enough to handle, divide it in about six lengths. Have children butter their clean hands, then pull the lengths of taffy until it is light and fluffy. Twist it into ropes of desired thickness. With kitchen shears, cut it into bite-sized pieces. Wrap each piece in wax paper. Makes two pounds.

Materials needed:

- 1 heavy saucepan
- 2 c honey
- 1 c sugar
- 1 c cream
- butter, softened (enough to grease pan and children's hands)
- 9" x 13" pan
- kitchen shears
- wax paper

Caution! Supervision required. Be extremely careful when using heat source.

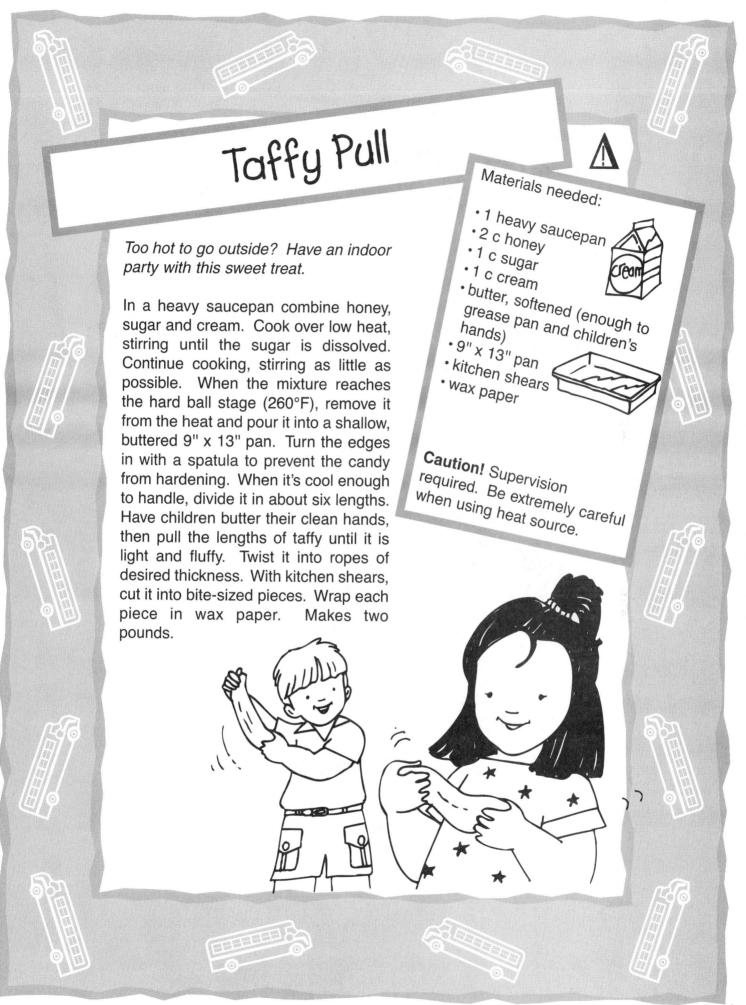

Summer Fans

Use these fancy fans to keep cool!

Have children use crayons or markers to decorate the construction paper. Then have them accordion fold the paper. Tape the bottom of the fan together, securing it with several layers of tape for a handle.

Garden Party Attire

Have an outdoor garden party with children wearing these bows.

Place the four layers of crepe paper on top of each other. Slide a bobby pin through all four layers, pushing the crepe paper to the end of the bobby pin. Shape it in a bow. Boys can wear these as bow ties, and girls can wear them as hair ribbons.

Materials needed for each child:

- 4 4" lengths crepe paper (various colors)
- bobby pin

Ladybug Racers

Children will enjoy making these and having their own races!

Have children paint their half walnut shells with black dots. Add eyes.

Make a ramp by leaning a board against a desk or table or use a plastic slide. Have children set their walnuts at the top of the ramp with a marble tucked inside each one. Then they let go of their ladybug racers at the same time and see who gets to the bottom of the ramp first!

Materials needed for each child:

- paintbrush
- acrylic paints
- 1 empty half walnut shell
- 1 marble

94

Butterscotch Crunchies

⚠

Materials needed:

- 1 heavy saucepan
- 1 12-oz pkg butterscotch chips
- $\frac{1}{2}$ c peanut butter
- 6 c cornflakes
- aluminum foil or wax paper
- scoop (optional)

Caution! Supervision required. Be extremely careful when using heat source.

These delicious no-bake treats won't heat up the kitchen on a hot afternoon!

Melt butterscotch chips and peanut butter together slowly. Mix in cornflakes until they're well coated.

Let children use a scoop or their fingers to drop the cookies on foil or wax paper. Refrigerate them for several hours, or keep them in a freezer and eat them frozen.

September

Apple Smiles

Materials needed for each child:

- 2 apple slices (red apples)
- peanut butter
- 1 plastic or butter knife
- 10 miniature marshmallows

These delicious and nutritious snacks look like real mouths!

Have children spread peanut butter on one side of each apple slice. Place the marshmallows on the peanut butter along the peeling edge of the apple slices to look like teeth. Put the apple slices together to form a mouth.

Grandparents' Day Cards

This unusual sandpaper card will be a hit with Grandma and Grandpa.

Fold the construction paper to make a card. Cut a piece of sandpaper the same size as the front of the card. With the pencil, sketch a picture on the rough side of the sandpaper. Color the picture, pushing down hard with the crayons. Use plenty of color.

Place the sandpaper picture on a cookie sheet. Put the cookie sheet in a 250°F oven for a few seconds and watch the crayon melt. Remove it from the oven and let the picture cool. Glue the sandpaper picture to the front of the grandparent card. Write a message inside the card.

Materials needed:

- pencils
- medium sandpaper (one sheet per child)
- crayons
- 1 cookie sheet
- construction paper or cardstock (one sheet per child)

Stamp-Art Stationery

Materials needed:

- colored paper
- stamps
- inkpads

Children can use their creativity to make their own stationery. This is ideal for writing letters to grandparents, to parents for Open House or to school personnel at the beginning or end of the school year.

Have children create decorative borders on sheets of paper using rubber stamps, leaving blank space for writing a letter. Have each child write a letter in the center of the stationery.

From: Tyler

Crowns

Children will love making, decorating and wearing these crowns.

Have children staple the paper strips together to make one long strip. Fold the coffee filter in half, and lay the center of the paper strip between the folded halves along the fold line. Glue the halves of the coffee filter together, with the headband strip inside. Decorate the coffee filter "crown" and headband by gluing stars and diamond shapes on it. Staple the two remaining ends of the headband strip together to fit the child's head.

Materials needed for each child:

- 2 1½" x 12" construction paper strips for the headband
- stapler
- 1 coffee filter
- glue
- scraps of colored construction paper for stars and diamonds
- scissors
- crayons or markers

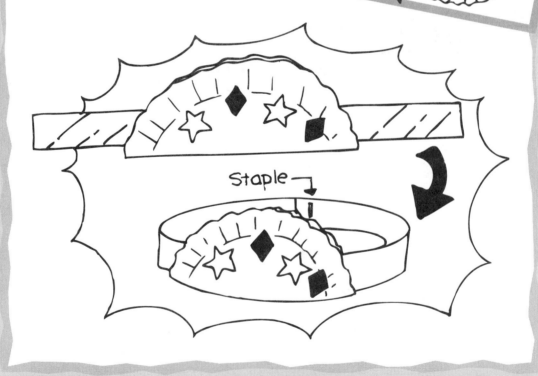

Staple →

Flowerpot Pencil Holders

Make this attractive pencil holder to give to Grandma, Grandpa or another special family member.

Cut a stem and leaves from green construction paper. Glue the wooden craft sticks all around the outside of the juice can. (White glue works well for this.) Push the sticks together tightly to completely cover the outside of the can.

HINT: You may want to glue one stick to each can ahead of time so that it will be securely in place when younger children begin to work on the project. They can use it as a guide.

Glue the stem and leaves on the side of the covered can. Glue the petit four cup at the top of the stem to make a flower.

Materials needed for each child:

- 4" x 4" square green construction paper (for stem and leaves)
- scissors
- 20 wooden craft sticks
- 1 six-oz juice can (washed and dried)
- glue
- red petit four cup

Streaming Sock Balls

Materials needed for each child:

- clean tube sock
- scissors
- several ribbons (different widths, lengths and colors)

Children will think that making this homemade toy is quite a "feet."

Cut off the top of the tube sock. (See diagram.) Cut the top into smaller pieces and stuff them into the toe of the sock. Tie pieces of ribbon around the opening to enclose the stuffing in the toe. Throw your ball in the air and watch the ribbon streamers flutter.

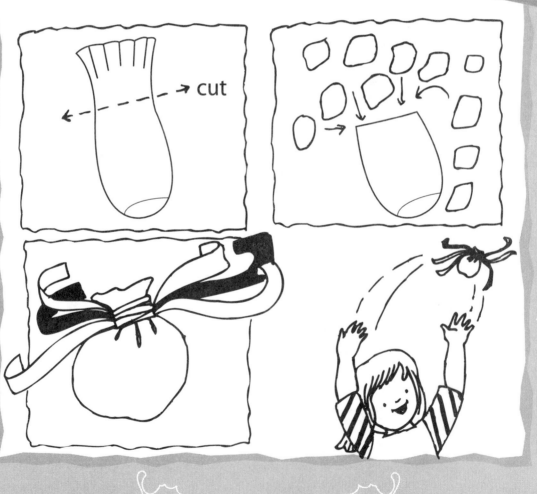

cut

Gift Bags for Grandparents' Day

Children will love making these cute gift bags to hold their homemade gifts for Grandma and Grandpa.

Fold over the top of the lunch sack about 3". Cut a roof, windows and door from construction paper and glue them on. Use a folded sheet of construction paper for the roof. Punch two holes through the top of the sack and roof and secure it with a ribbon.

Materials needed for each child:

• brown paper lunch sack
• colored construction paper
• scissors
• white glue
• hole punch
• ribbon

Cat Gift Bags for Grandparents

This cute gift bag can hold a special gift for Grandma or Grandpa.

Enlarge the cat pattern below. Lay the cat pattern on a collapsed lunch sack and cut around it. Cut the feet and legs apart. Glue the bottom and sides together. Leave the top open. Punch a hole in the top and insert ribbon for a handle.

For Nana and Papa

Cherry Graham Cracker Pudding

A delicious and easy treat to make!

Mix the vanilla pudding and milk according to the package directions. Pour it in a pan. Mix the cherry pie filling with the pudding. Let the children break the graham crackers into tiny pieces. Add them to the mixture and serve the treat. Yum!

Peanut Butter Candy

⚠️

Materials needed:

- 1 c peanut butter
- 1 c maple syrup
- 1 c powdered milk
- mixing bowl
- wax paper or serving tray

These delicious treats are easy to make, and no baking is required.

Mix peanut butter, maple syrup and powdered milk together. (Add more powdered milk or syrup, if needed, for the desired consistency.) Let children roll the mixture into balls and place them on wax paper or a serving tray.

October

Dancing Spiders

Children will enjoy making these spiders to hang up for Halloween decorations.

Give each child eight strips of black construction paper for the legs. Have children curl each strip by rolling it on a pencil. Stack the strips on top of each other and poke a brad through the top to hold them together. Secure the brad and spread the legs out. Glue yellow eyes on two of the legs near the top. Tie a length of yarn around the top of the brad and hang it from the ceiling.

Materials needed for each child:

- 8 spider legs made from black construction paper cut into 8" x 1" strips
- yellow construction paper
- brad
- pencil
- yarn

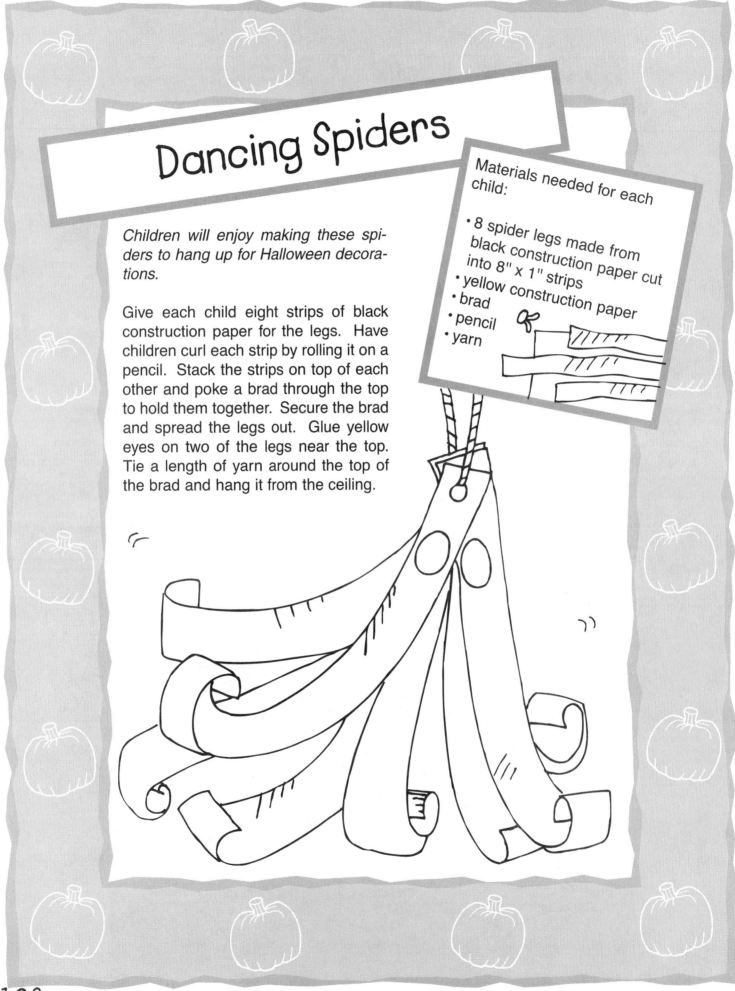

Dancing Jack-o'-Lanterns

Children will fold, trace, cut, glue and staple to make this seasonal door decoration.

Cut a pumpkin shape from the orange construction paper. Have the child draw a face on it with black marker, then glue on a stem cut from green construction paper. For hair, add green curling ribbon. For arms, accordion fold 12" x 2" strips of black construction paper. For legs, accordion fold 18" x 2" strips of black paper. Have children trace their hands and feet on yellow construction paper. Cut them out and glue or staple them to the accordion-folded arms and legs. Glue or staple the other end of the arms and legs to the pumpkin.

Materials needed for each child:

- large sheets construction paper (orange, black and yellow)
- scissors
- black marker
- 1 small sheet construction paper (green)
- glue
- green curling ribbon
- stapler

Shrunken Heads

These faces made from dried apples can look really scary—the perfect thing for a Halloween party. Older children can make these themselves, but you may need to help younger children.

Materials needed:

- apples
- apple peeler or small knife
- $\frac{1}{2}$ c lemon juice
- 2 tsp salt
- whole cloves
- few grains of uncooked rice
- wire rack

Peel a large apple and coat it with a mixture of lemon juice and two teaspoons of salt to prevent browning. With a potato peeler or small knife, carve eye sockets, a nose, mouth and ears out of the apple. (Don't bother with small details. They will be lost when the apple dries. Go for big features and nature will take care of the rest.) Stick in whole cloves for eyes and raw rice grains for teeth.

Set the apples on a wire rack in a warm, dry place for about two weeks. Let the children check their apples every day to watch them shrink!

Rice Cake-o'-Lanterns

Children can create their own nutritious, delicious edible jack-o'-lanterns.

Give children rice cakes. Add yellow and red food coloring to strawberry-flavored cream cheese to make it orange. Let children spread it on their rice cakes, then add candy corn for jack-o'-lantern eyes, nose and mouth.

Materials needed for each child:

- rice cake
- strawberry-flavored cream cheese
- yellow and red food coloring
- 6-7 pieces of candy corn
- plastic knife

Lollipop Ghosts

Materials needed for each child:

- lollipop
- 1 white facial tissue
- yarn or ribbon
- black marker

Children won't be frightened by these simple, edible ghosts.

Have children cover lollipops with facial tissues, then tie yarn or ribbon around the base of the lollipops to divide the ghost "head" from the "body." They can each draw a face on it with the black marker.

Curly Tail Black Cats

Children will enjoy creating this cat with a curly tail.

Using the patterns, cut the head, body, tail, ears and whiskers from black construction paper. Glue the head to the body. Glue the ears on top of the head. Cut two large eyes from white construction paper and two small pupils from black. Glue the black pupils on the white eyes, then glue them on the cat. Cut a nose from pink paper. Glue the nose on the cat's head. Draw the mouth. Glue the whiskers on. Glue the curly tail to the body, as shown.

Materials needed for each child:

- patterns, page 114
- construction paper (black, pink and white)
- scissors
- glue

Curly Tail Black Cats Patterns

head

body

eye–Cut two.

pupil–Cut two.

whisker–Cut eight.

ear–Cut two.

nose

tail

Ghostly Piñata

Children will enjoy having this as a part of their Halloween festivities.

Have children help you draw a face on the trash bag using the sealed edge as the top of the ghost. Fill the bag half full of small toys and wrapped candy. Tie a string tightly around the center. Poke two holes near the top of the bag and tie a long rope through the two holes. Use the rope to hang the piñata over a tree branch, swing set or similar place. The open end of the trash bag will look like the tail of the ghost. Have children hit the piñata with a plastic bat until the bag breaks and the contents fall out.

Materials needed:

- 1 white, kitchen-size, plastic trash bag
- black marker
- small toys and wrapped candy
- string
- rope
- plastic bat

Papier-Mâché Jack-o'-Lanterns

Children will learn to follow steps in a process as they create these jack-o'-lantern decorations.

Blow each child's balloon up and tie it. Create a paste of flour and water. Have children dip strips of newspaper in the flour paste, then press the strips firmly onto their balloons until they are thoroughly covered. Let them dry for a couple of days. Spray each newspaper-covered balloon with orange spray paint. Let it dry. Have children cut eyes, nose and mouth from yellow construction paper and glue them on their jack-o'-lanterns.

Materials needed for each child:

- balloon
- old newspaper
- flour
- water
- orange spray paint
- yellow construction paper
- glue

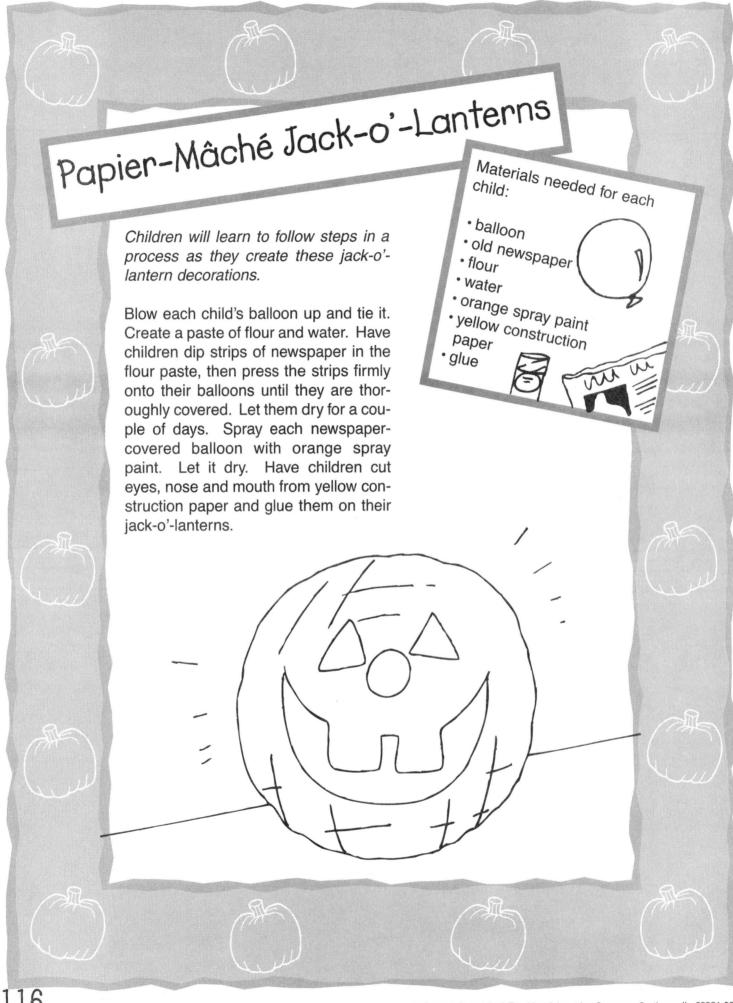

Spooky Spiders

These spiders will get any room ready for Halloween.

Place the egg cup on old newspaper, and cover it, inside and out, with a coat of black acrylic paint. Use the end of a paper clip or tack to poke four holes along the bottom of both sides of the cup.

To make fuzzy legs, cut four black pipe cleaners into 7" lengths. Thread a pipe cleaner through one of the holes, into the cup and out the corresponding hole on the other side. Make sure the ends protrude an equal length from both sides of the cup. Bend them upward to make legs. Fold them downward to create knees. Bend them again near the tips to make feet. Glue on the googly eyes.

Materials needed for each child:

- 1 egg cup from a cardboard egg carton
- old newspaper (or another surface for painting)
- black acrylic paint
- paintbrush
- tack or paper clip
- 4 black pipe cleaners
- googly craft eyes
- glue stick

Pumpkin Punch

Children will enjoy making this delicious orange drink!

Let children help mix orange sherbet and lemon-lime soda in a punch bowl. Enjoy the treat!

Materials needed:

- 1 punch bowl
- 1 two-liter bottle lemon-lime soda
- 1 pt (or more) orange sherbet

Witch Puppets

Children can make these puppets and have a Halloween puppet show.

Cut the witch's chin and face from light green construction paper. Glue the chin under the flap on a brown paper lunch sack. Glue the face to the top of the flap. Have children curl black or green curling ribbon (by running it along a scissors blade). They can glue it on the sides of the face for hair. Cut a hat from black paper and glue it on top of the head. They can each put a hand in the bag to make the witch "talk."

Materials needed for each child:

- patterns, page 120
- construction paper (light green and black)
- scissors
- glue
- 1 brown paper lunch sack
- black or green curling ribbon
- crayons or markers

Witch Puppet Patterns

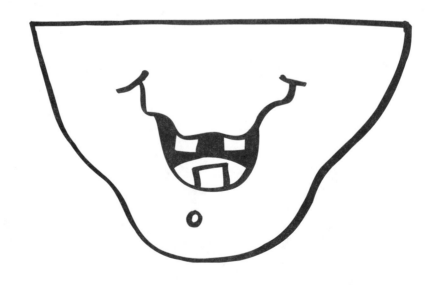

Halloween Hands

Children will love making these creepy but delicious Halloween hands.

Have each child open the glove by putting a hand inside. Then have the child drop one candy corn, pointed tip down, into each finger of the glove. Fill the glove with popcorn, leaving enough room to tie a bow at the top with yarn. This makes a great decoration that can be eaten later!

⚠️

Materials needed for each child:

- 1 clear plastic glove
- 5 pieces of candy corn
- popcorn
- yarn

Fall Wreaths

Go on a fall drive to collect these items ahead of time, or take children on a nature walk to gather items for their wreaths.

Have children glue leaves and small pinecones on the cardboard base to make wreaths. Let them dry, then hang them for decorations.

Materials needed for each child:

- 1 round doughnut shape cut from cardboard, to use as wreath base
- fall leaves, pinecones, acorns and other autumn objects
- glue

Napkin Rings

These napkin rings can be used at place settings for a classroom party or at home on Thanksgiving.

Cut a piece of crepe paper to fit around the tube section. Put a line of glue all around the top and bottom of the tube section and glue the crepe paper to it to make a napkin ring. Let it dry. Stick a Thanksgiving sticker on the ring for a decoration. Place a napkin through the ring.

Materials needed for each child:

- 1 1" wide circle from a cardboard tube
- green, brown or orange crepe paper
- scissors
- glue
- Thanksgiving stickers
- 1 paper napkin

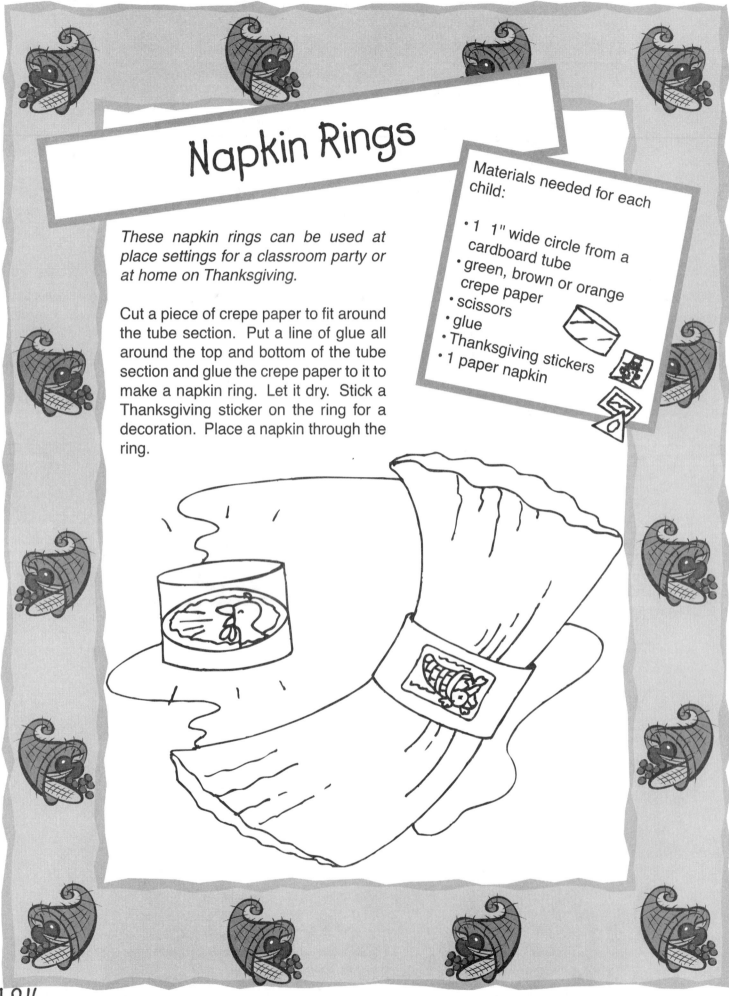

124

Turkey Place Mats

Children can practice following directions as they assemble this place mat to use for a classroom party or at home on Thanksgiving.

Cut a large oval shape from brown construction paper for the turkey's body. Cut feather shapes from yellow, red and orange construction paper and glue them on the body to make the tail. Cut a small oval shape from light brown construction paper for the turkey's head. Draw eyes and a beak on the head. Cut a wattle from red paper and glue it under the turkey's beak. Glue the head in the center of the body, as shown in the sketch. Cut two turkey feet from yellow construction paper. Glue the top edge of the feet to the bottom edge of the turkey body. Laminate the turkey with clear, self-adhesive plastic to protect it when you use it for a place mat.

Materials needed for each child:

- 9" x 12" sheet brown construction paper (for the body)
- scissors
- yellow, red and orange construction paper (for feathers)
- glue
- crayons or markers
- 9" x 8" sheet light brown construction paper (for the head)
- 2" x 4" piece red construction paper (for the wattle)
- 3" x 7" sheet yellow construction paper (for the feet)
- clear, self-adhesive paper for laminating (optional)

Turkey Mosaics

Children will use their individual creativity in making this decorative turkey mosaic.

Create a pattern for children by enlarging the turkey below on cardstock. Use the marker to trace the turkey pattern on cardstock or cardboard. Draw eyes and mouth. Then cover the turkey with glue. Place beans, peas, rice and corn all over the turkey. Press them down to make sure they stick.

Materials needed for each child:

• 1 sheet cardstock or cardboard
• black marker
• pinto beans, rice, peas, lima beans, corn and other dried food items
• glue

3-D Turkeys

Materials needed for each child:
- 2 Styrofoam™ balls (one small and one medium)
- 3 toothpicks
- feathers (real or from a craft store)
- 2 googly craft eyes
- glue
- 1 small piece of red felt
- craft clay

Children can use motor skills to assemble these free-standing turkeys.

Attach two Styrofoam™ balls together, one for the body and one for the head, using a toothpick to connect them. Stick feathers into the body (medium Styrofoam™ ball). Glue the eyes to the head (small Styrofoam™ ball). Cut a small triangular piece of red felt and glue it under the turkey's chin. Insert two toothpicks into the bottom of the body for legs. Put small balls of craft clay onto the legs for feet.

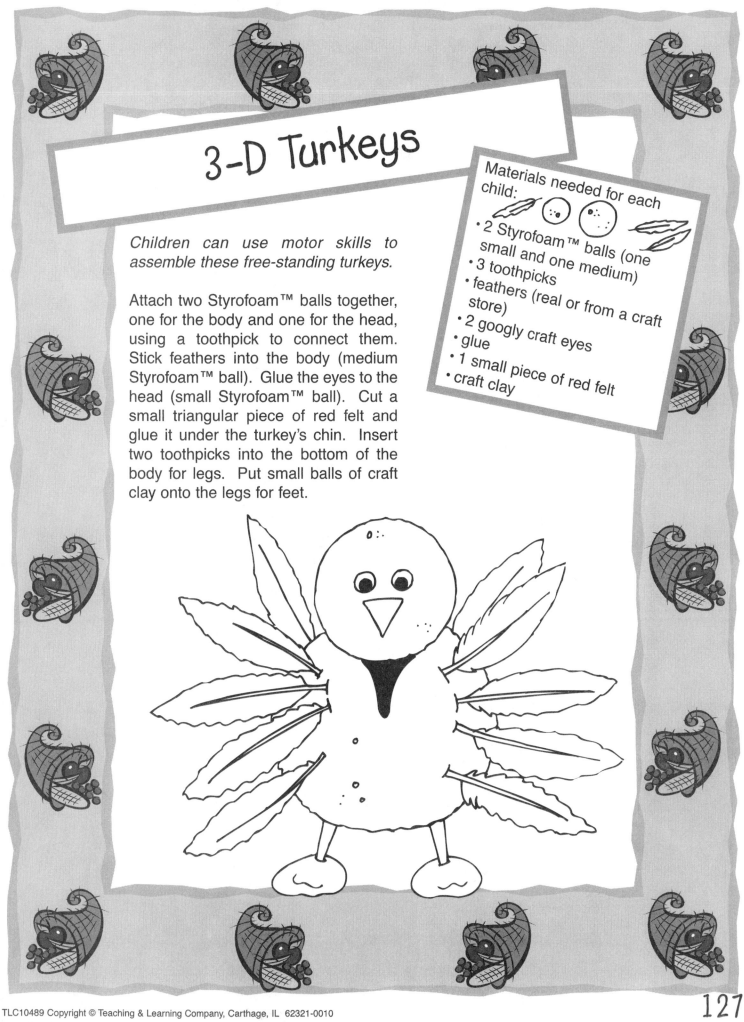

Mr. Curly Tail Turkey

Cut the turkey body from brown construction paper. Draw a face on the turkey. Cut 10 feathers from various colors of construction paper. Curl each paper feather around a pencil, then glue it to the turkey's back. Cut two feet from orange construction paper and glue them to the bottom of the body.

Materials needed for each child:

- patterns, page 129
- brown construction paper (for body)
- scissors
- crayons or markers
- red, green, yellow and orange construction paper (for feathers and feet)
- pencil
- glue

Gobble

Gobble

Gobble

Gobble

Mr. Curly Tail Turkey Patterns

body

feather

feet

Finger-Paint Turkeys

This tactile project turns turkey into a finger food!

Have each child dip a whole hand in one paint color and press it onto a clean sheet of paper. Let it dry, then use crayons or markers to draw a face for the turkey on the thumb. Or the child may press each finger into a different color of paint, then press it on the paper to give the turkey multicolored tail feathers.

Materials needed for each child:

• finger paint (various colors)
• 1 sheet white paper
• crayons or markers

Brett

Winter Sparkles

Celebrate the onset of winter activities with this outdoor art project.

Pour about 1" of water into the margarine tub. Lay the evergreen branch in the water in the bottom of the tub. Make a circle from the string by tying the ends together. Place the knotted end of the string in the water in the tub, and drape the rest of the loop over the edge of the tub. Carefully put the tub in the freezer. When the water is frozen, carefully remove the ice "ornament." (You may need to run warm water over the bottom of the tub.) Hang the "sparkle" outdoors where it can catch the light of the sun.

Materials needed for each child:

- water
- 1 plastic margarine tub, washed and dried
- 1 small evergreen branch, leaf, twig or other "nature" object
- 1 length of string

Happy Scarecrows

Lots of cutting, gluing, drawing and stapling will make a darling scarecrow head.

Cut two oval head shapes from a flat, collapsed paper grocery bag. Staple together the edges of the two ovals to make a head, leaving an opening for filling. Fill the scarecrow head with newspaper or toilet paper. Staple the opening shut. Cut two triangle eyes from blue construction paper and glue them on the scarecrow head. Glue on a button nose. Draw a red mouth. Cut two red cheeks from construction paper and glue on. Cut yellow strips from construction paper, and glue them to the sides of the head for straw hair. Cut a hat from orange construction paper. Decorate the hat with fabric scraps cut into small rectangles with pinking shears. Glue the hat on the scarecrow's head.

Materials needed for each child:

- 1 brown grocery bag
- scissors
- stapler
- old newspaper, paper towels or similar stuffing material
- blue construction paper
- glue
- 1 button
- red crayon or marker
- construction paper (yellow and orange)
- fabric scraps

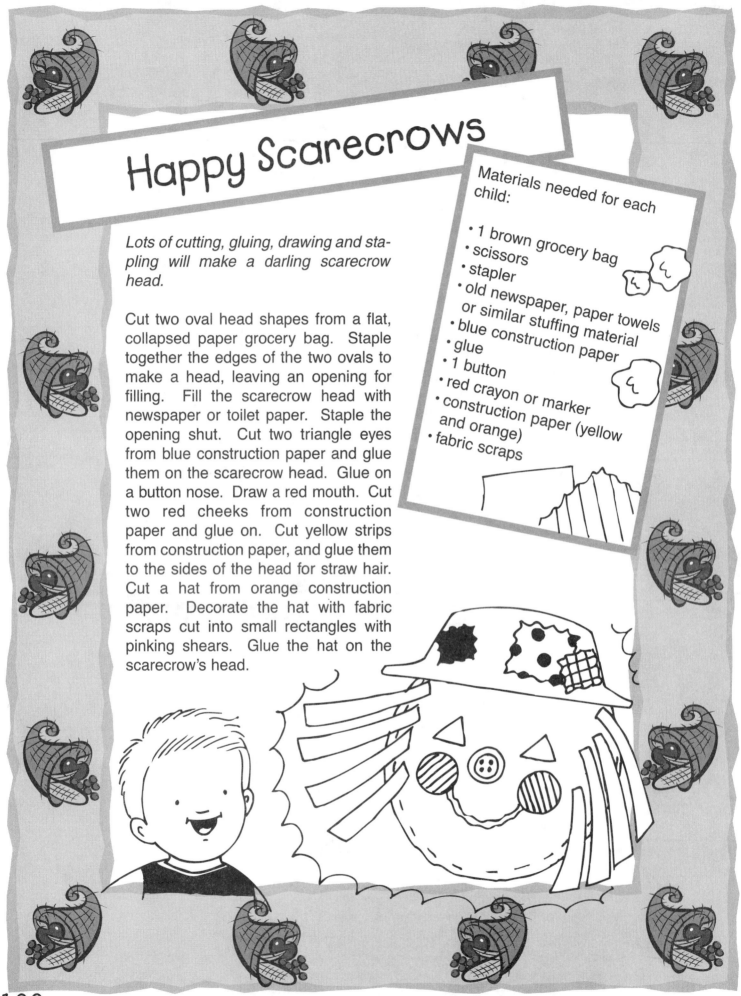

December

Pinecone Christmas Trees

This is a fun craft that involves painting with glue. Lots of fun!

Have children "paint" the pinecones with glue, then before the glue dries, sprinkle it heavily with green glitter. Top it with a paper star cut from yellow construction paper. When the pinecone dries, glue on sequins or tinsel.

Materials needed for each child:

- 1 pinecone
- glue
- paintbrush
- green glitter
- yellow construction paper
- scissors
- sequins or tinsel

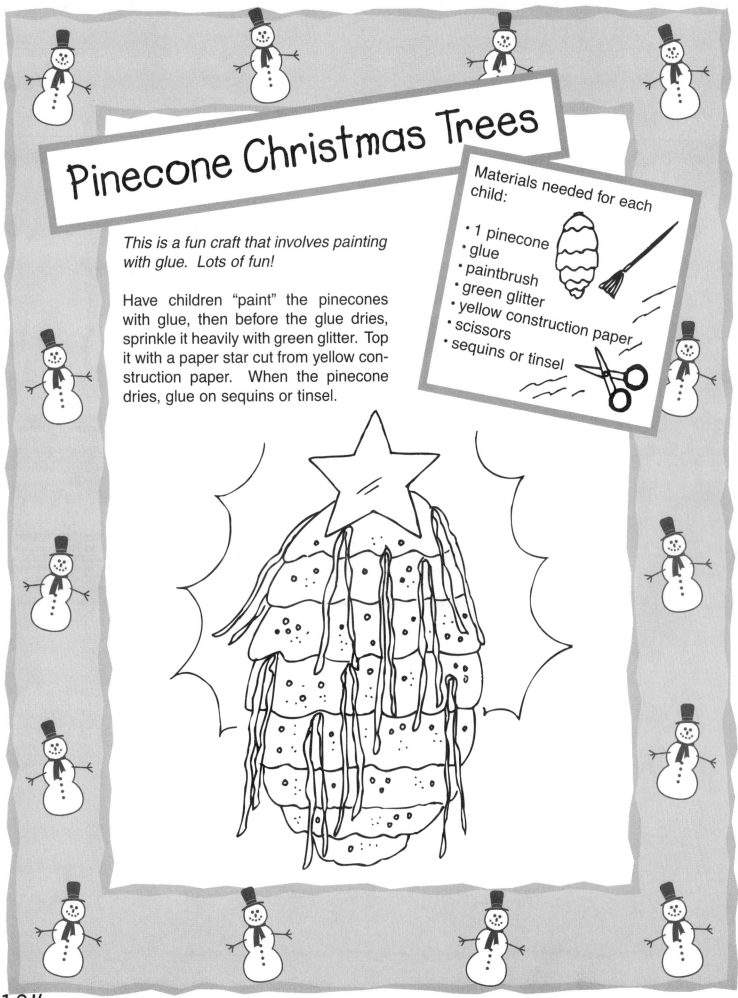

Candy Cane Reindeer

These are a cute little holiday decorations, and they're easy to make.

Leave the wrapping on the candy cane. Glue the eyes on the rounded curve of the candy cane. Glue a pom-pom under the eyes for a nose. Tie the ribbon into a bow on the straight part of the candy cane just under the nose. Wrap one of the pipe cleaners around the crook of the candy cane, just above the eyes, to begin the antlers. Cut the other pipe cleaner in half and use these pieces to embellish the antlers.

Materials needed for each child:

- 6" candy cane, wrapped in cellophane
- 2 googly craft eyes
- glue
- 1 red or brown pom-pom
- ribbon
- 2 pipe cleaners

Juice Can Lid Ornaments

Make beautiful ornaments from objects found around the house.

Using the juice can lid as a pattern, trace and cut a circle from construction paper. Follow the same procedure to cut a round picture or a small silhouette from a holiday card to fit on the paper circle. Glue the picture on the paper circle. Glue the paper on the can lid. Glue a ribbon around the outside edge of the lid. Have an adult use a glue gun to attach a paper clip or ornament hook to the lid for a hanger.

Materials needed for each child:

- 1 juice can lid, washed and dried
- scissors
- construction paper
- old holiday greeting cards
- glue
- ribbon
- 1 paper clip or ornament hook

Caution!
Supervision required. Be extremely careful when using heat source.

Pasta Christmas Wreaths

A classic holiday art project to treasure!

Cut the center out of the paper plate. Glue dry pasta noodles around the outer ring, completely covering the paper plate to make a wreath. Let it dry, then spray-paint the entire wreath. Have an adult use a glue gun to add the bow.

Materials needed for each child:

- 1 small paper plate
- scissors
- variety of dry pasta shapes
- glue
- silver or gold spray paint
- bow

Caution! Supervision required. Be extremely careful when using the glue gun.

Beaded Candy Canes

These are fun and easy to make, and a great way to teach patterns to young children.

Slip the beads onto the pipe cleaner, one at a time in an alternating red-white pattern, a multicolored pattern or randomly with multicolored beads. Twist the ends of the pipe cleaner to keep the beads in place.

Materials needed for each candy cane:

- 1 pipe cleaner
- beads (red and white or multicolored)

138

Clothespin Reindeer

Children enjoy making these little reindeer, then playing with them.

Make a pattern for children from the deer shape below. Cut out the reindeer shape from construction paper. Have children draw on a face and paint white dots on the body. They can attach clothespins for legs.

Materials needed for each child:

- 1 sheet brown construction paper or cardstock
- scissors
- markers or crayons
- white paint
- paintbrush
- 2 clip clothespins

Salt Dough Ornaments

Children can help you mix and shape the dough, or you can do it ahead of time and let the children paint the finished ornaments.

Mix flour, salt and water in a bowl. Knead the dough on a board until it's soft but not sticky. Roll the dough to about 1/2" thick. Cut out holiday shapes with cookie cutters. Using the toothpick, poke a 1/4" hole near the top of each shape for hanging. Place the dough shapes on a foil-covered cookie sheet. Bake at 275°F for about two hours. Check them periodically—the ornaments are done when they are completely dry. Remove them from the oven to cool. Let children paint the ornaments with acrylic paints. When the paint is dry, put a piece of string or ribbon through the hole, and tie the ends together to make a loop for hanging each ornament.

Materials needed:

- 2 c flour
- 1/2 c salt
- 3/4 c water
- mixing bowl
- bread board or similar kneading surface
- rolling pin
- cookie cutters
- toothpick
- aluminum foil
- cookie sheet
- paintbrushes
- acrylic paints
- string or narrow ribbon

140

Cornflake Wreaths

Children will love making and eating these edible wreaths!

In a large saucepan melt margarine over low heat. Add marshmallows and stir until they are completely melted. Remove the pan from the heat. Stir in the food coloring. Add cornflakes cereal and stir until it's well coated.

Using a $1/4$-cup dry measuring cup coated with cooking spray, evenly portion some warm cereal mixture onto a paper plate for each child. Have them shape the cereal mixture into wreaths with clean hands. (Buttered fingers greatly help this process.) Dot the wreaths with cinnamon candies. Add a bow of thin red licorice whip.

Materials needed:

- $1/2$ c margarine
- 1 10-oz pkg (about 40) marshmallows
- 1 tsp green food coloring
- 6 c cornflakes cereal
- red cinnamon candies
- 1 thin red licorice whip per child
- vegetable cooking spray
- saucepan
- $1/4$ c dry measuring cup
- 1 paper plate per child
- butter (for children's fingers)

Caution! Supervision required. Be extremely careful when using heat source.

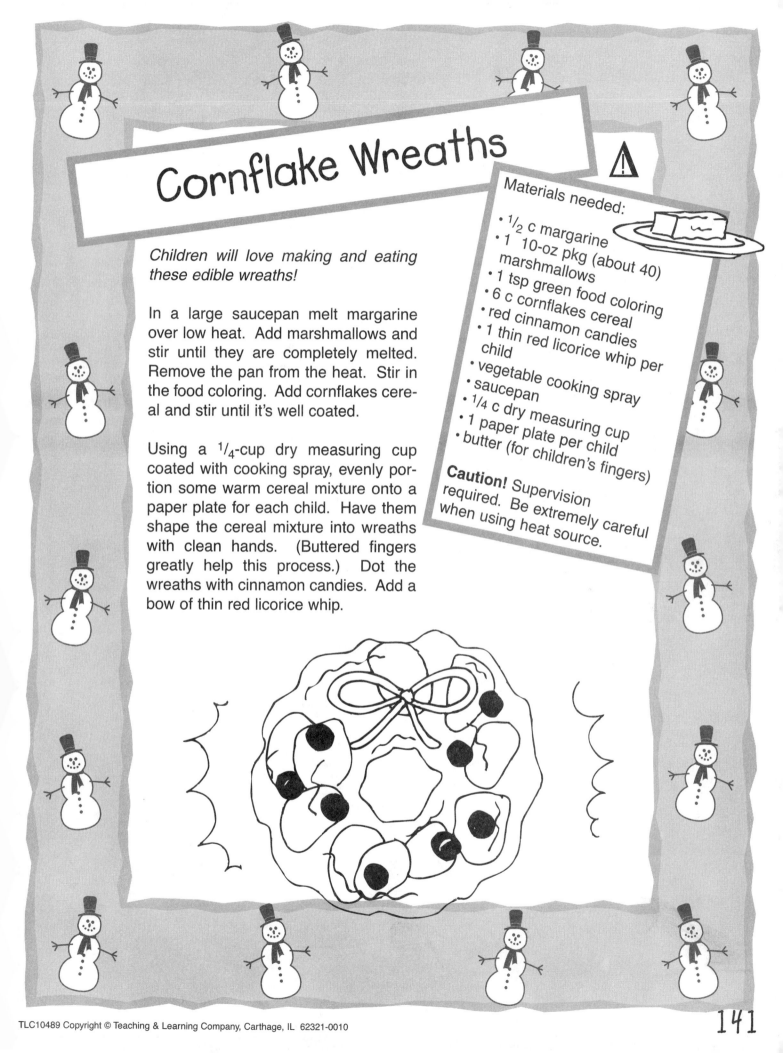

Lace-a-Stocking

Children can practice lacing while making these homespun stockings.

Fold the red construction paper in half. Draw a stocking outline on one of the halves. Cut through both layers of paper to make two stockings. Hold or clip the stockings together while you punch holes evenly around the sides and bottom. (The holes should be at least $3/8$" from the edge so the paper does not tear during the lacing process.)

Tie one end of the yarn to one of the holes at the top of the stockings and have the child lace the yarn through the holes to connect the stockings. Tie the other end of the yarn to the last hole through which you lace the yarn.

Let each child write his or her name vertically on the stocking with markers or glitter pen. Pull gently on the cotton balls to stretch them flat. Glue the cotton across the top of the front stocking. Fill the stocking with treats.

Materials needed for each child:

- 12" x 18" sheet red construction paper or cardstock (for the stocking)
- pencil
- scissors
- paper clips (optional)
- hole punch
- 36" length of green yarn
- 2 cotton balls (for the top of the stocking)
- markers or glitter pen

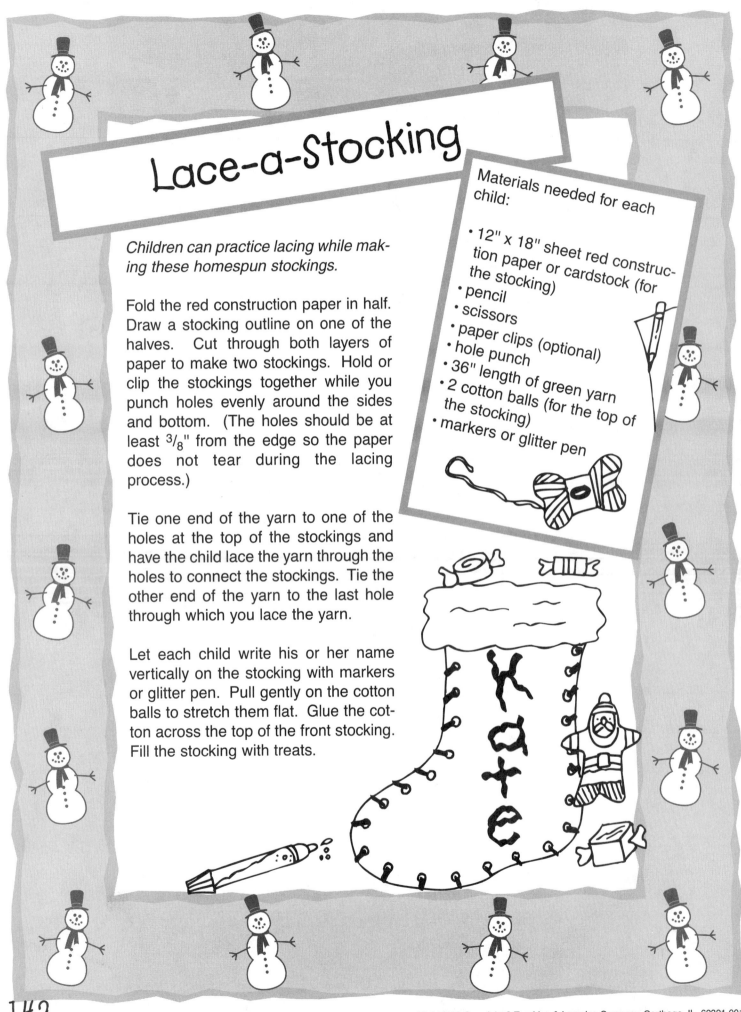

142

Reindeer Sandwiches

These sandwiches look like reindeer and are nutritious, too.

Make a peanut butter-and-jelly sandwich. Cut it diagonally to make a triangle for the reindeer's head. Put a dab of peanut butter on the sharp left point and stick a maraschino cherry half on it for the nose. Stick on a raisin for the eye and a piece of a pretzel for the antler. Break the pretzel apart to get an antler shape. (You only need one antler because the reindeer is in side view.)

Materials needed for each child:

• 1 paper plate
• 2 slices wheat bread
• peanut butter
• jelly or jam
• knife
• 1 maraschino cherry
• 2 raisins
• pretzel knots

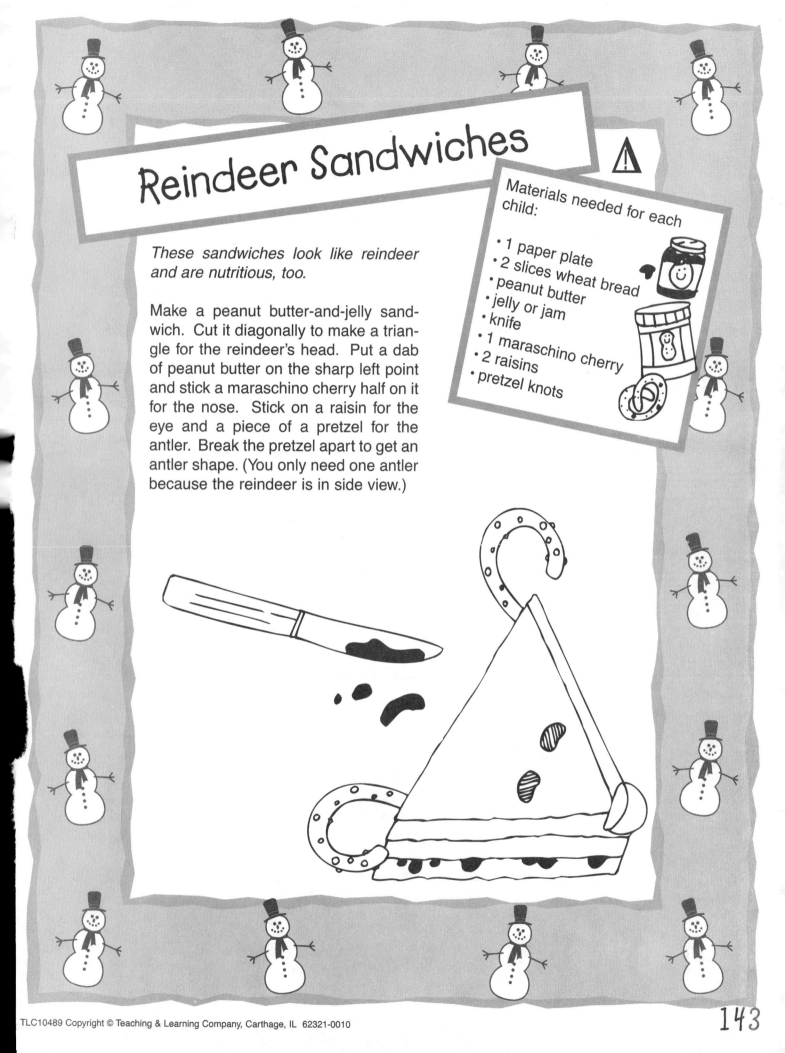

Fuzzy Polar Bears

Making these delicious treats is a fun winter activity.

Stirring constantly, melt chocolate chips in a saucepan over medium heat.

Insert a toothpick into a marshmallow, dip it into the chocolate, then roll it in the coconut. Place the marshmallow on a sheet of wax paper and remove the toothpick. Let it cool before eating. Make lots!

⚠️

Materials needed:

- 1 bag chocolate chips
- saucepan
- spoon
- toothpicks
- marshmallows
- shredded coconut
- wax paper

Caution! Supervision required. Be extremely careful when using heat source.